The Happiness Plan

Keys to a Fuller, More Positive Life

James D. Baird

LIGUORI
PUBLICATIONS

One Liguori Drive
Liguori, Missouri 63057-9999
(314) 464-2500

Imprimi Potest:
James Shea, C.SS.R.
Provincial, St. Louis Province
The Redemptorists

Imprimatur:
Monsignor Maurice F. Byrne
Vice Chancellor, Archdiocese of St. Louis

ISBN 0-89243-343-4
Library of Congress Catalog Card Number: 91-60236

Cover design by Pam Hummelsheim

Dedication

To my wife, Ellie. By her unselfish devotion, she gave me the best memories of my life's journey. She was a constant reminder and living example of our Lord's commandment to love others as we love ourselves.

Contents

Introduction

How This Book Came To Be

The incentive for this book came from a radical change in my value system. After dedicating the majority of my life to the pursuit of material success and achieving that goal, I realized that it wasn't worth the sacrifices I'd made. My time and efforts totally revolved around business, to the exclusion of my family and friends. There was little or no time for relaxation, fun, or spiritual development. My state of mind could best be described as tense, stressed, and grim. Laughter and play were never considered. Negative thinking became my way of life.

Then, in my late fifties, two shifts developed that changed my life's purpose. First, my business began generating an income that adequately supported my needs and desires while demanding very little of my attention. More importantly, my mortality began to press in on me. The value of my material success was diminished to an insignificant level when I realized the limited time left to me between now and eternity. How to use this time became my primary focus. The conclusion was clear; there wasn't even a close second choice. My life would be spent in practicing happiness and preparing for eternity.

Not surprisingly, happiness and preparing for eternity are one and the same. The reason is simple: if one is happy, what could be better than an eternity of happiness? Viewed from the criterion of inner joy (detailed in the first chapter and expanded throughout this book), I had lived an unfulfilling life, had a loveless childhood (perhaps genetically predisposed), and had developed a stressful business career. Although I had been blessed with a loving wife and wonderful children who gave me great pleasure, I was to learn that happiness (joy) comes from within rather than from others. I was to learn that happiness is pure gift.

Devoting my energy to the research of happiness, I concluded that happiness is not only available to everyone but also is a direct result of meeting our Creator-designed needs. Our Creator fashioned us to gear our lives toward meeting three intrinsic needs. To the extent we satisfy these needs, we are happy — in this world and eternity.

My conclusions are based on the truths of Scripture, personal experience in life, and various spiritual and human-development writers. My conclusions are supported with convincing scientific documentation. I am an inventor-engineer and a pragmatist. "If it doesn't work, redesign it until it does" is my natural bent. Consequently, a primary specification for pursuing happiness is to develop something that works, that's practical, and that readers can comprehend.

I bring my own history to bear on these reflections. I have gained a knowledge of materialism; I have experienced firsthand a movement from hunger to wealth, from a loveless childhood to a loving family, from assets of zero to millions, and from an unhappy, godless life to a spirit-filled inner joy that transcends any previous happiness. I lived the life of worldly success and have sampled the joy of the Spirit.

My writing style is intended to be informal: that form of communication we use when talking with our friends.

Consequently, major conclusions without mountains of supporting evidence will frequently be used in an attempt to make the material practical for most readers.

These directives for happiness will work for those of us who have oversubscribed our time to too many goals and priorities. The plan starts with a daily time commitment of twenty minutes and grows as we realize the fruits of our initial efforts. Each movement toward meeting our needs has its own reward; we feel encouraged to form happiness habits that will direct our lives according to our Creator-inspired design. Our thoughts and actions become directed toward meeting these needs.

Regardless of our walk of life, our wealth or lack thereof, our level of education, our physical characteristics — or anything else — we have been imbued by our Creator with certain intrinsic needs. They are universal to every human creature and give a natural direction to our life energies. To encourage us to move in the right direction, our Creator opens to us simple pathways of wholeness and goodness. If we move in the right direction, we know growth toward wholeness; when we move in the wrong direction, we suffer pain and brokenness. This book attempts to help the reader plan movement in the right direction, which in turn glorifies our Creator.

If the previous statements seem to oversimplify life, perhaps we've made life too complex in the first place. Human beings have examined every detail of life, from every angle, over thousands of years, using billions of minds and countless words and thoughts. Yet the meaning of life and its purpose are simply and clearly contained in the Scriptures. Just as the Master Teacher taught with simple words and thoughts, this book, too, is presented in uncomplicated words and statements. Wisdom springs from simplicity.

Happiness ways are not a new discovery or an inspired revelation. Rather, these truths are revealed in the Scriptures. I present them here in today's language and supplement them with the latest relevant research and schools of thought. After all, simple truths have lasting impact on our lives; the rest gets lost in the complexity and diversity of humankind's new and changing thoughts. Like the truths of our Lord, the way to happiness never changes. It was this way for the first person on earth; it's the same for us today. Because of God's unconditional love for all human creatures, we've been fashioned with certain intrinsic needs that provide meaning and purpose to our lives. We know that Jesus was happy; he was the personification of all the goodness he taught. That happiness is available to us as well.

Any errors in the presentation of this plan are, of course, my own. While I offer my best effort, I take comfort in knowing that our Lord is more concerned with my intentions than ultimate results. It is said, "You teach what you want to learn"; in this regard, I experienced considerable satisfaction in researching and writing this book. While the work is seriously dedicated, I have an incurable inclination toward whimsy laced with a sense of dry humor. This sometimes pops through at the most inopportune times. For this I apologize. Hopefully, it does not offend or distract you on your journey toward happiness.

Our Three Intrinsic Needs

T he premise of this book is that all humans are formed and fashioned by their Creator with three intrinsic needs. Perhaps this was done to promote natural order and harmony consistent with the nature of our Creator, to glorify God through all things. To increase the glorification, we are also gifted with free will, thus preempting robotic responses. The divine plan is channeled to us through these needs. In turn, we exercise our free will by devoting our life energies to fulfilling these Creator-designed needs. These intrinsic needs, which are the same in nature for all humans, motivate us to the glorification of our Creator, which brings the highest meaning to our lives. To the degree we fulfill these needs, we know the happiness of inner joy.

Because happiness is primarily generated from within ourselves, it is available to all of us provided we are physically, emotionally, and spiritually able to meet our intrinsic needs. We must be in control of our minds and claim an active belief in God. This is not to say that those not in control of their minds are not happy; some enjoy a special state of grace. Such circumstances, however, are beyond the scope of this book.

No matter what other gifts of a mental or physical nature we may have, and regardless of our wealth, social status, cultural opportunities, stage of life, and so on, our intrinsic needs remain the same. Individuals vary, of course. The quality and quantity of the need to be loved, for example, is unique to the individual. The need, however, is basic.

We spend our lives, to our last breath, attempting to meet these needs. The central obstacle to happiness is the attempt to meet our inner intrinsic needs with outer materialistic action. Consequently, no matter how hard we try, we will remain unfulfilled and dissatisfied. Increasing the effort only intensifies the anxieties to a point of stress and destructiveness. Decreasing the effort, we resign ourselves to suffering, complaining, and surviving with whatever brief pleasures we manage to eke out.

The purpose of this book is to explain the nature of our intrinsic needs and to explore ways to fulfill them, thereby living complete and happy lives for which our Creator designed us. The source reference for this theory is a matter of scriptural interpretation; the proof of the interpretation is how the theory works in our lives. "The proof of the pudding is in the eating." The proof of the happiness plan is realized in the inner joy discovered. First, we must understand the nature of the three basic intrinsic needs.

Intrinsic Need 1: To love and be loved. Love is one of humankind's most powerful words. Whatever its interpretation to the individual, love generally means something positive and desirable. Our Creator etched our genes, formed our minds, coded our DNA, or by some other means beyond our imagination instilled in us the need for love. Some of us need a large amount in constant doses; others manage with smaller rations. The rest of us are in the middle. Without a sufficient amount of love to fulfill our individual love need, however, happiness escapes us.

Fortunately, God has gifted us with the means to fulfill our love need by giving us the capacity to receive unconditional love. We have but to learn how to accept God's unconditional love. Once we accept God's love, we learn to love ourselves and others. God is the Creator and source of all love. We simply take that love into ourselves and spread it around. Since God is the original supplier, the supply is unlimited. It never wears out or deteriorates; rather, it is self-magnifying and self-perpetuating. We know we're unconditionally loved by God: "For God so loved the world that he gave his only Son, so that everyone who believes in him might not perish but might have eternal life" (John 3:16). God's love is an unearned gift to all creatures. There is nothing we can do to be worthy of or earn this gift; it is given without condition.

Intrinsic Need 2: To live a meaningful life. We need to believe that we are accomplishing a meaningful and worthwhile purpose in our lives. What makes us feel important varies considerably from person to person. Ruler or slave, billionaire or welfare recipient, sales clerk or sales manager, director of the board or lunchroom janitor: all is irrelevant. Satisfying this need has to do with belief in ourselves and our life direction. God has a plan for each of us, a plan which fulfills our purpose in glorifying him. Jesus had such a plan or mission in his life. His final words were "It is finished" (John 19:30). He knew the satisfaction of having fulfilled his mission in life.

As to what God has planned for our lives, we cannot foresee, but we are graced with the capability to move in the right direction. When we enjoy the process of meeting our self-determined goals, we're probably on the right path. When we enjoy a sense of accomplishment, this is probably a good sign. When we're happy to share our giftedness with others, this is the right way. Finally, when we actually enjoy the privilege of serving others, our ways are in accordance with the intentions of our Lord's teachings. If our life plan is not directed toward serving others and is basically self-serving, it will not glorify God; we will not meet our purpose in life or fulfill our intrinsic needs. Those who have spent their lives building self-serving power, wealth, security, or fame have not tasted the inner joy of fulfilling this need.

Intrinsic Need 3: To care for the body. The body is the temple of the Spirit. The care, feeding, and maintenance of the body is an essential support function serving to help meet the first two needs. Any top performance requires a combination of a healthily trained mind and body. When the body is unhealthy, the mind is proportionately distracted from meeting the first two intrinsic needs. Much of what happens to the body due to the aging process, certain diseases, accidents, and so on, is beyond our control. On the other hand, through diet, exercise, and thought control, we can delay the effects of the aging process and retard or eliminate the effects of certain diseases and accidents. We can directly effect preventive maintenance of the body by the elimination of unhealthy habits that impair or destroy its proper functions. Recent medical research gives us sound instruction for health maintenance. As we grow older, the body plays a smaller part in happiness; the importance of the power of the mind becomes more significant.

The remainder of this book is devoted to further study of these intrinsic needs and exploring ways they can be met — ways that glorify God and foster our own sense of self-goodness and happiness. A chapter is devoted to each of the intrinsic needs: what they are and how to fulfill them. Chapter IV is devoted to daily living: "Practicing Happiness." I propose a plan of action for forming new habits that align with fulfilling our intrinsic needs. Chapter V focuses on the human need for support. When everything seems to go wrong, we look for special encouragement. Chapter V offers that encouragement.

Finally, personal reflection pages have been provided for your own insights and prayers.

Definitions

At the outset it's important to understand the use of key words: love, spirit, and happiness. If we're not using the same meaning, generated thoughts will lead to different conclusions, our path to happiness may take a wrong turn, and we might get lost. The following definitions are not the first listings in *Webster's Dictionary;* they are, however, the ones intended by Jesus.

Love: Love has so many meanings that it's said to be indefinable. Perhaps that is so from a total perspective, but we're interested in Jesus' perspective. Jesus urges us toward the love called *agape.* The other kinds of love in the Greek language of the New Testament are *philia, storge,* and *eros.*

Agape is of the will; it involves doing God's will by seeking another's welfare. *Philia* is of the emotions and takes delight in another's presence. *Storge* is an instinctive concern for a blood relative; it often includes *agape* and *philia. Eros* is of the flesh as well; in marriage it is part of the divine plan and contributes to a successful marriage. These distinctions will be explored more fully in the first chapter.

Spirit: There are many and diverse meanings for spirit in today's vernacular. For our purposes we speak of the Spirit as "a supernatural being or essence." Unless otherwise noted, the word *Spirit* refers to the "essence of God," the Holy Spirit. "I will ask the Father, and he will give you another Advocate to be with you always, the Spirit of truth, which the world cannot accept, because it neither sees nor knows it. But you know it, because it remains with you, and will be in you" (John 14:16-17). In the same way, Jesus describes the Holy Spirit. The Bible also makes references to evil spirits as manifestations of the devil, but they are not dealt with in this book.

Happiness: Of prime importance, of course, is the word happiness. Since the purpose of this book is to achieve a higher level of happiness, we obviously need to agree on its meaning. Webster defines happy as "good luck or fortune; a state of well-being, contentment, and joy." Joy is defined as "the emotion evoked by well-being, success, or good fortune" and "the experience of great pleasure or delight." Joy seems to be a more intense state of happiness.

In none of the common definitions is there any reference to the duration of the condition of happiness or joy — and therein lies the major difference. The goal of pursuing happiness is to achieve a state of mind that ensures a perpetual state of well-being and joy dependent on the eternal truths of God. The idea is to revise the TGIF (thank-God-it's-Friday) attitude — wherein we suffer all week for the pleasures of the weekend — to a more constant state of happiness.

Therefore, genuine happiness must come from within ourselves, like the Holy Spirit, and be a function of something unchanging, like God. We will refer to *happiness* as "a level of well-being and joy, proportional to the fulfilling of our Creator-designed intrinsic needs."

Eternal Guarantee

The happiness plan is guaranteed to work for a lifetime, for eternity. The Guarantor is the only one who can back up such a claim. This is an unlimited warranty available to all who follow the divine design. Our Lord intended for us to be joy-filled and happy, a truth referenced over two hundred times in Scripture. A few examples indicate our Lord's desire and intention for us to be joyful and happy:

"If you keep my commandments, you will remain in my love, just as I have kept my Father's commandments and remain in his love.

"I have told you this so that my joy might be in you and your joy might be complete."

(John 15:10-11)

The fruit of the Spirit is love, joy, peace, patience, kindness, generosity, faithfulness.

(Galatians 5:22)

"Until now you have not asked anything in my name; ask and you will receive, so that your joy may be complete."

(John 16:24)

For the kingdom of God is not a matter of food and drink, but of righteousness, peace, and joy in the holy Spirit.

(Romans 14:17)

Chapter I

Intrinsic Need 1:
To Love and
Be Loved

The Virtue of Perseverance

P erseverance implies that we exert all our energies to achieving a goal regardless of the obstacles. Jesus is our primary example of perseverance. No matter the price, nothing deterred him from his goal; no matter the adversity, he did not detour from his mission.

To persevere you must believe in yourself, have a good self-image, forgive yourself for past mistakes, and not fear the mistakes you will make in the future. In short, perseverance must be generated from love.

The quality of perseverance is determined by the value of the goal. The human being can be driven by power, lust, fear of failure, and so on, and can persevere for a limited time with limited obstacles. Perseverance for the world-class goals in this life and the next, however, can only come from love. For love casts out fear of failure, grants forgiveness, and ensures a belief in the goodness of one's goals.

My purpose in these pages is to offer direction in pursuit of the goal of happiness — an attainable goal that will require a great deal of effort, time, and energy. The goal is a worthy one, however, and the pursuit is indeed worthy of our perseverance. Joy of the Spirit awaits us.

Joy of the Spirit

W hat is the joy of the Spirit proclaimed in the Scriptures? Is it intellectual satisfaction? the feeling of completing a job well done? No. Joy is the exhilaration of the soul. It ranges from a slight to an intense feeling that pervades the body, bubbles over, and makes us want to share it with others; its intensity can be more than any external pleasure known to humankind. Since joy is internally generated, it is available to anyone who would know goodness and follow the ways of Jesus.

It is sad that some worldly seekers of pleasure spend untold hours, effort, and money attempting to acquire brief and self-diminishing pleasures when internal and self-perpetuating joy can bring lasting happiness. Inner joy never leaves one with a hangover, regrets, or apologies; rather, a warm afterglow of happiness tends to linger at some deep level until the next exhilaration occurs. The frequency of these experiences varies from person to person depending on their respective spiritual and physical efforts to meet their intrinsic needs.

Opportunities for us to know the joy of the Spirit are endless. This is our greatest gift after life itself and God's unconditional love and eternal presence. No earthly pleasure comes close to the joy of accepting God's love. If we could only realize that we often seek happiness in the wrong places, our Christian conversions would be immediate, complete, and transformational.

Spiritual Development

Transformation is the gateway into spiritual growth and development. Transformation is a movement toward being at one with God, whether it's resolving a conflict between body and mind or making a conscious move toward the development of virtues. One moves from one level to another by climbing the stairs a step at a time. The inner way is a life plan shaped by a conscious desire to be at one with God, a life plan built around a set of disciplines that allows one to transcend self-centeredness and develop a special knowing, loving awareness of the presence of God.

Transformation is not a mere matter of change, however. We can struggle to change in many ways, only to find ourselves returning to old habits. But when transformation takes place, things change without effort. Old habits evaporate; new beliefs and habits take over. Life becomes charged with inner energy and excitement.

Inner transformation is like waking from sleep and realizing that God is everywhere, in everything; God's will and your life plan are clear. Your spiritual aspirations become the major object in your life.

As you travel the way of spiritual growth, however, beware of spiritual pride. In pursuing spiritual growth, some believe that engaging in constant acts of holiness will move them up an ever-ascending staircase toward God. But it is God's grace that empowers us to deeper spiritual living. Only through God's gifts to us, rather than through any special abilities of our own, do we move closer to God and know life more abundantly.

In addition to spiritual pride, there are other pitfalls: going to extremes and getting out of balance with the reality of everyday living. Becoming fascinated by faith healers, prophets, preachers, and evangelists who have a hypnotic appeal in the name of God, for example, are all potential traps. Authentic teachers of the inner way warn against being "turned on" by psychic phenomena that occur from time to time. The test of time proves the worth. If emotional fireworks are of a worldly nature, they will fizzle. If they are of God, they will linger — often a lifetime.

A start toward spiritual development is spiritual communication through meditation and prayer. The first requirement of meditation is silence, and the purpose is to reveal you to yourself; in silence you discover your mind and body. You can then build on this awareness by practicing a series of exercises. As you continue these exercises, you begin to discover your true inner self; you grow to like your true self more and more. At some point, you realize that God is meeting you in your centered self where the silence is filled with the sound of God's still, small voice. It is only in the cushion of silence that you can hear your inner self.

Begin by sitting comfortably for several minutes at a time. Gradually increase this time over the course of several weeks. Although your mind will continue to race through everyday problems, your body remains still. A basic exercise is to shift your attention to your body, letting yourself feel the sensations of body awareness. Examine these sensations. The apostle Paul said, "Do you not know that your body is a temple of the holy Spirit within you, whom you have from God, and that you are not your own? For you have been purchased at a price. Therefore glorify God in your body" (1 Corinthians 6:19-20).

Spiritual growth calls for respecting your body's

needs: nutrition, exercise, rest, recreation, and hygiene. You care for your body not out of pride or anxiety about health but out of love and admiration for the temple of the Holy Spirit.

Be aware of your breathing as well. Imagine that the air you breathe in is God. Breathe God in; breathe God out. Be aware of that and stay with that awareness. Prayer can be as simple as breathing. In doing this, you pray not only with your head but also with your heart. You move from *thinking about* God toward *being present with* God. Ultimately, in the experience of that presence, you find yourself loving God with your whole heart. Learn the techniques of relaxation so you can move at will into the calmer and more peaceful states of consciousness found during the tranquil moments of meditation.

This is the first exercise — and perhaps the hardest — on the road to spiritual growth. It requires a shift of attention from the head to the heart. Relaxation combined with sensory awareness is a proven process for meditation. This involves moving out of the normal high level of brain activity, where you do your rational thinking and decision-making, to the decreased level of activity of alpha, where a peaceful, present tranquillity is experienced. This slows down the rational activity of the brain and leaves it more open to creativity and receptivity. There is no application of prideful, rational thinking that requires proof and evidence. The mind opens; the soul becomes quiet and accepts God in the way a child might. This condition of acceptance is essential. After all, God is not knowable to our intellect, only to our hearts.

We will come to taste a sweet surprise in this accept-ance: God is not about making us smart, pure, or power-ful. Rather, God is about making us loved and loving human beings. In God's presence we are cleansed, redirected, wakened, empowered, and bonded to him and to all people. With wholehearted loyalty and devo-tion, our hope rests not in our love for God but in God's love for us. Our goal in spiritual growth, therefore, is not to love God initially but first to be willing to accept God's unconditional love. We must open ourselves to God, relax our fears, and experience the presence of God in all of life around us.

Why the Good Suffer

When tragedy strikes, one of the most frequently asked and unanswered questions is "Why me?" When it happens to the righteous, it's even more puz-zling. How can a loving, perfect God do such horrible things? Indeed, many turn away from God when they feel themselves to be innocent victims; they vent their anger on God for abandoning them.

Most of us were raised believing that one gets what one deserves. After all, Scripture reads, "Make no mis-take: God is not mocked, for a person will reap only what he sows" (Galatians 6:7). And in many situations, it's reasonable to see that we often deserve the misfortunes following irresponsible or inappropriate choices. How-ever, when the reaping is disproportionate to the sowing, this analogy fails.

Another concept often proposed is that we are a sinful species, that we are getting our just desserts for the sins of humankind. God's punishment falls not only on the sinner but also on his or her descendants through the generations. "You shall not bow down before them or worship them. For I, the LORD, your God, am a jealous God, inflicting punishments for their fathers' wickedness on the children of those who hate me, down to the third and fourth generation but bestowing mercy, down to the thousandth generation, on the children of those who love me and keep my commandments" (Deuteronomy 5:9-10).

At best, these answers are attempts to provide some consolation and reduce suffering; at worst, they are the efforts of those in theological positions to retain their power by having all the answers. Each explanation calls for further reflection.

The theory that people are just getting what they deserve can't be correct. It can't be true that bad things happen to good people because we all bear the cross for the sins of humankind. This negative thinking causes people to blame themselves for everything bad that happens to them. People end up disliking themselves, their God, and others.

Obviously, this premise is also at odds with the teachings of Jesus. Jesus taught love: love of God, ourselves, and others. Our most primary Creator-fashioned need is to love and be loved. The life of Jesus was one of positive thinking and action. Negative, unjustified guilt had no place in the Good News Jesus proclaimed. Generations ago, guilt was a common tool used by some religions to control congregations. In the mass communications of today, however, and with the present level of awareness, fear and guilt don't work. People flock to congregations that preach love, positive thinking, and personal goodness. The fact that this style of religion is popular and trendy doesn't necessarily make it theologically perfect, of course, but it does make it practical. What's important is to make Jesus' way come alive today for the good of all humankind. Preaching styles and ceremonies come and go; the Word of God lives on.

We've dismissed the notion that righteous suffering is God's vengeance for humankind's sins. But imagine a God who isn't interested in humankind, and unjust suffering is merely a matter of chance. Or imagine that the universe as we know it is just a small event in the big picture of life and eternity, that there is long-term meaning we can't grasp. From God's viewpoint, perhaps all is consistent and in harmony with some master plan. Senseless suffering for unknown sin is a heavy cross to bear, but if this suffering is somehow a contribution to God's design, the burden seems lighter, perhaps an honor.

Still, none of these theories are in harmony with the nature of God's unconditional love.

Job's Wisdom

The Book of Job addresses in great detail the subject of good people suffering. In light of our previous discussion, we can put forth several premises in an attempt to understand the Book of Job.

- *Job is good.*
- *God is just, and the good will be rewarded and the sinful will be punished.*
- *God causes everything that happens.*

The characters in the Book of Job tend to believe these three statements. In the end, however, Job accepts his suffering by realizing that we live in an unjust and imperfect world. Many readers of this book of the Old Testament are predisposed to believe that God causes all things to happen. In reality, bad things happen to good people; bad things happen to bad people; bad things happen to all people. They just happen. There are reasons for bad things occurring, from our own direct choices to statistical probabilities. Many misfortunes are predestined by our style of thinking: negative thinking.

The bottom line is that we need to take responsibility for our lives. We cannot blame God or ourselves, in other than premeditated cases, for our suffering. Rather, we should freely turn to God in the pain and pray for comfort and help.

Free Will

T he divine plan provides for free will, the freedom that allows us to cause suffering in ourselves and others. The drive for power, by some, is the ability to cause discomfort to others. Any time power is exercised, there will be some level of suffering to someone.

Yet free will is a cornerstone of the divine plan. It is that condition which gives meaning to the glorification of God — the purpose of life. As free will gives us the latitude to do good or evil, it also allows us to cause pleasure or suffering in ourselves and others.

Think Like Jesus

In summation of the above discussion, we understand that bad things happen because

- *Free will allows us to hurt ourselves and others*
- *Negative thinking predestines negative events*
- *God does not cause everything in our lives*
- *Careless accidents occur*
- *Statistical probabilities exist;*
  natural phenomena exist

In all cases, we need to turn to Jesus. The more we think like Jesus, the more we reduce the chances of bad things happening to us and others. Self-love, love of others, and body care are crucial. For bad things that are out of our control, Jesus is our answer. He offers comfort to the suffering and strength to bear any cross.

God did not create us to wander around in aimless suffering. Rather, we were created in God's image to use our free will to glorify God and love ourselves and our neighbors. No one said it would be easy. If it were effortless, where would be the glory for God? In enduring life's bad things while fulfilling our intrinsic needs of love, we come to know spiritual joy in this world and eternal happiness in the next. There is no other choice worth considering.

Forms of Love

I n an earlier discussion we noted four meanings of love as the Greeks understood the word: *agape, philia, storge,* and *eros.* We add *lust* to the list.

Agape: In the relationship of one person to another, *agape* is "the unselfish concern for the good of another." This is the kind of love to which God commands us; it is of the will, not of the emotions.

Philia: This form of love delights in another's presence, and as such, cannot be commanded. *Agape* and *philia* can coexist, and in fact, this is highly desirable since their coexistence means we can do God's will with delight.

Storge: Persons who are blood relatives usually experience a strong form of love called *storge.* It is basically instinctive.

Lust: The Hollywood-type romance promoted by the media is an example of a type of love that is self-centered and of a physical and biological nature alone. This kind of attraction is referred to as *lust.* Its sole object is to seek its own momentary pleasure.

Eros: Love of the flesh in marriage is part of God's divine plan and depends on the type of love called *eros.* As the relationship matures, *eros* matures into a spiritual form which moves toward *agape* and centers on the needs of the other person.

In all following discussions, we use the word *love* to mean *agape.*

Growth in Love

M odern day uses of the word love often are confined to those types of romantic interludes associated with soap operas, romantic novels, and scandal sheets. Unfortunately, the word is commercialized and distorted beyond scriptural meaning.

The love God commands is *agape,* which is of the will, and can be achieved by all regardless of our emotions. *Agape* can well be enhanced by the emotional attraction of *philia.*

The reason there is love in our hearts in the first place is so we can love our Creator and all creation. Under certain circumstances, love of the flesh *(eros)* is part of the divine plan, and as one becomes aware of love, its more mature form becomes spiritual. This is beautifully demonstrated in the stages of a successful marriage when the initial stages of erotic love bloom into a deeper, less self-centered love concerned with the needs of the other.

Selfless love is basically spiritual and is a continuing

awareness of the other person's needs. Selfless love requires work and is continually tested. As one successfully weathers a crisis and expects smooth sailing, another wave appears. After enough of these experiences, one gains confidence in the integrity of the relationship and is able to meet future problems with greater measures of selflessness. A couple becomes secure in the knowledge that by strengthening their bond in life's small problems, their love is tempered to survive crises.

Let Go of Sadness

S adness has no redeeming qualities in the choice to love. When sadness sets in, it feeds on its own despair, distorting our thinking toward a negative viewpoint. Logic fails as our sense of reality becomes confused by pessimism. Loving acts aren't even considered as we judge our brothers' and sisters' acts to be hostile. Aggression is the usual response.

Sadness is the opposite of joy, like day and night. They can't coexist. Sadness has no discernable benefits and destroys or damages the lives of untold millions. Because it is our nature to strive for happiness, we strike out at our adversary in the wake of sadness. Frequently, we look for immediate pleasures such as alcohol or carnal delights, or we try to escape through frenzied activities — all in an attempt to distract our attention while, hopefully, the sadness passes. While the sadness may be temporarily alleviated by the distraction, it remains nonetheless; its cause hasn't been eliminated.

Since no rational-minded human being would choose sadness, we are driven in the direction of joy. One of the quickest and most successful methods, of course, is to pray and meditate. As we pray, we begin to view things more from an eternal perspective; our daily problems seem less urgent. Our act of prayer confirms our dependency on God. Only when we fully realize and accept this dependency can God's healing affect us. Once God's unconditional healing love is accepted, sadness cannot remain, for love banishes sadness as surely as day follows darkness.

Regardless of power, fame, fortune, or any other circumstance, no one can remain independent of God and be happy. If we do not acknowledge our dependency by prayer, we have no chance of discovering God's gift of happiness. For prayer instigates goodness, and to know goodness is to know God and accept love. Accepting our dependency on God's love is the basic substance of inner joy that replaces sadness.

Be Forgiving

In its more developed form, failing to forgive can be a complete block to happiness. When it develops into a state of anger, it causes a production of bodily chemicals. Except in the relatively rare instance of an emergency (fight or flight), these chemicals cause unpleasant side effects. They can lead to tension, vascular headache, irregular heartbeat, stomach pain, peptic ulcer, diarrhea, and other unpleasant conditions.

Failure to forgive and the violent forms of anger which result are like diseases that you invite to attack you. Failure to forgive is self-punishment. It is negative and serves no useful purpose. You get mad at someone, probably over a perceived injury to your pride, the chemicals flow, your body feels bad, your mind is blocked with a negative attitude, good thoughts are prevented, sadness develops, and adding insult to injury, the person you're mad at doesn't feel a thing. No one benefits.

On the other hand, forgiveness is a form of self-love. It is a positive gift of the Spirit available to all who will accept it. Forgiveness of self is often more difficult than forgiveness of others but just as essential to your health and happiness. Our Lord taught us to pray: "Forgive us our debts, as we forgive our debtors" (Matthew 6:12).

Eliminate Guilt

We are all familiar with feeling guilty for things we've done in the past. Like anger, guilt is a negative attitude that bears only bad fruit. What possible profit is there in torturing ourselves over past mistakes?

Guilt is like a spreading disease that destroys us spiritually, emotionally, and physically. Our Lord understood this. He said that we should forgive not seven times but seventy times seven. Thus, there should be no limit to the forgiveness we extend to ourselves and others.

Guilt over the past and fear of the future are two restrictions on a healthy self-image. But both restrictions dissolve when we accept God's unconditional love. We learn to correct our actions through the experience of our past mistakes, and we forgive ourselves for making the mistakes in the first place. Fear is put to rest by accepting the peacefulness of God's love. "There is no fear in love, but perfect love drives out fear because fear has to do with punishment" (1 John 4:18). We repent of our sins while God has already forgiven us. Can we do less?

Pride and Humility

P ride is a root cause of all sin because it pushes us from God. With knowledge, for example, one can wield power over others. Yet knowledge, in itself, is neither good nor evil. Only when we use it for power, control, and ego-building do we pridefully sin. This is also exemplified by the person who derides the learned, thereby attempting to build himself or herself up while eroding the integrity of others.

This prideful ambition to use knowledge as a gimmick for our own needs forces out humility; wisdom and truth are blocked. The affirmation of the ego and the artificial puffing up of one's worth are counterproductive to happiness. The more the ego asserts itself, the more unhappy we become.

Humility, on the other hand, is the recognition of the truth of ourselves. It is not an effort to demote or subjugate ourselves, to show ourselves unworthy. We simply know ourselves to be loved by God through no effort of our own. Our goodness and worthiness are innate, and the humble person knows this.

Loneliness and Love

Loneliness, the unfulfilled need for love, is a part of all of us. For many, it's a great burden. The root of loneliness is a refusal to accept God's love. We must give love to receive love, yet we must have it in order to give it. The starting point is God: accepting that God loves us and then learning to love ourselves.

Some choose loneliness because of the risk involved: the fear of rejection, the fear of being taken advantage of, the fear of being mocked. In pursuit of happiness, however, there is no choice — for what are we if we do not love? "If I have all faith so as to move mountains but do not have love, I am nothing. If I give away everything I own, and if I hand my body over so that I may boast but do not have love, I gain nothing" (1 Corinthians 13:2-3). Life without love is no life at all. Without love we do not glorify God and thus have no real purpose in life.

God loves us unconditionally; we are God's creation. Since God's very nature is love and we are created in that image, God obviously loves us. And if God loves us, we must be immeasurably lovable. Once we accept this reality, we have love to return to God and reflect to others. This chain of belief in love tends to multiply love: the more we give, the more is returned. If we are lonely, it is our choice. God's grace of love is ours; joy and happiness are ours. We have only to accept it all. Any risk we take to gain love and reduce loneliness is of no real consequence compared to the gain. After all, what do we actually risk other than injury to our pride? And even that is to our advantage, since the result of pride is alienation from God. That which we risk losing we are better off without. In turn, we gain love, the essence of life. The choice of loneliness or love is not difficult to make.

Why Worry?

The world has been in turmoil since the beginning of time. Anxieties and catastrophes are our inheritance. How to live in the turmoil of today and keep peace of mind is the subject of countless articles, books, and seminars. However, the only source of authentic peace is Jesus. "Peace I leave with you; my peace I give to you. Not as the world gives do I give it to you. Do not let your hearts be troubled or afraid" (John 14:27).

Basically, peace is the product of realizing that anxieties have no worth or profit; they are totally negative. All the worrying in the world improves nothing and in reality only serves to worsen the situation by negative thinking. This understanding is intellectually achieved by a few, but most of us need the help of Jesus to put worrying into proper perspective, as is the case with most worldly concerns. When we look back on our life experiences, what do all the worries add up to? We probably can't remember a fraction of them.

Catastrophes have always been with us. Thanks to modern technology, we are made painfully aware of the plight of our global sisters and brothers. As our awareness expands to include the tragedies in remote Third World countries as well as local tragedies, our anxiety potential swells. Today, many of us live in a tension-charged world in emotional turmoil without spiritual quiet. As we torture ourselves with anxieties and worries, we become fearful: how will we cope with all the problems that may beset us? Anxieties are fuel for phobias and neurotic obsessions. All of this unnecessary emotional turmoil takes over the mind and leaves no space for spiritual peace.

The consequences? a person in a state of emotional and/or physical suffering wandering without direction. Time for prayer and meditation becomes short, shorter, extinct. Slavery to worry becomes a way of life. The continuous noise of humankind's anxieties rings in the brain, pushing out the quiet that is needed for the Word of the Lord.

What to do?

First, insist on a daily period of prayer and meditation. This will put a brake on escalating anxieties. During this time, turn all anxieties and worries over to God. When problems are more imagined than real, or beyond our realistic ability to solve, turn them over to God. Taking an eternal perspective on life often gives worries their proper value: zero. When we contemplate the cosmos of eternity, daily worries pale significantly. For those of us who are not so philosophical, Chapter IV will be helpful.

We must ultimately realize that worry serves no purpose, cannot help, and may in fact hurt us. We must realize that worry is nothing more than a form of self-punishment. Jesus instructed us not to worry: "Do not worry about tomorrow; tomorrow will take care of itself. Sufficient for a day is its own evil" (Matthew 6:34).

In addition to daily quiet time, schedule time for fun and exercise. For some, these are one and the same; for others, they bear no relation whatsoever. In any event, both fun and exercise help to rest our minds from worry and anxiety. We are given a chance to meditate on reasons not to worry.

Replacing the worry habit with prayer, meditation, fun, work, and exercise is a direct path to happiness.

Egotism and Happiness

Today's culture encourages the ego to dominate others in an attempt to satisfy our own self-centeredness. While encouraging the ego is an effort to meet our intrinsic needs of love and a sense of self-worth, it is misdirected. For this reason it does not satisfy those needs. Self-assertion of the ego fails to produce happiness; in fact, the more we assert our ego, the more miserable our condition becomes.

Everyone who swells his or her ego pushes farther and farther away from the Lord. The ego's satisfaction is never complete; yet, attempting ego satisfaction gives continual rise to excess. Humility becomes more difficult as one's material desires increase; the ego swells and tends to block out spiritual wealth. It may be for this reason that Jesus spoke of the difficulty of the rich entering the kingdom of heaven.

Pride and egotism do not bring happiness, inner peace, or any kind of spiritual sweetness. What a huge mistake to devote one's life to collecting perishable earthly treasures at the cost of happiness on earth — and possible loss of happiness for all eternity.

Holiness and Happiness

Quieting the ego and resisting the invitations of materialism are lifetime struggles. The very reality of a humble life resists cultural reasoning. Those who have trusted humbly in God's unconditional love and have fashioned their lives with spiritual values, however, have discovered the treasures of both happiness and holiness. Reason played no role in their choices; they merely accepted their intrinsic need to love and be loved.

Models of this courage abound. Someone like Mother Teresa speaks to us of acceptance, humility, and spiritual wealth. The life of such a person produces love, joy, peace, patience, kindness, generosity, forbearance, gentleness, faith, courtesy, temperance, and purity: all gifts and fruits of the Spirit. These characteristics are the result of fulfilling Intrinsic Need 1. These characteristics embody an entire attitude toward life itself.

The Be-attitudes of Life

I n his Sermon on the Mount, Jesus describes certain attitudes that lead to happiness, attitudes that condition us to meet our intrinsic needs. These attitudes are not of the world but of the Spirit. When they are embraced as part of our natural orientation toward life, they foster inner joy.

"Blessed are the poor in spirit, for theirs is the kingdom of heaven" (Matthew 5:3). We all know ourselves to be spiritually poor to some degree. When we acknowledge this reality by accepting our dependency on God and trusting that God loves us unconditionally, we discover happiness. Unhappiness results when our intrinsic needs are not met; and our intrinsic needs are not met when we depend on ourselves rather than God.

"Blessed are they who mourn, for they will be comforted" (Matthew 5:4). Why do bad things happen to good people? The fact is that bad things happen to all people; they're just more noticeable when they happen to good people. We often blame ourselves, others, or God for the bad things that happen to us. In some cases, misfortune is the direct result of our own poor or irresponsible choices. In other cases, the misfortune that occurred today had its origins generations ago. In any event, our God is a God of love. We can count on that love to comfort us in our mourning. Through these trials our faith will be strengthened.

"Blessed are the meek, for they will inherit the land" (Matthew 5:5). Humility is simply knowing and accepting the truth about ourselves. It is not an exaggeration; it is not an understatement. It is an expression of our true selves, who we are in the sight of God. Happiness is the inheritance of those who acknowledge the truth.

"Blessed are they who hunger and thirst for righteousness, for they will be satisfied" (Matthew 5:6). Our Lord said, "So do not worry and say, 'What are we to eat?' or 'What are we to drink?' or 'What are we to wear?'... Your heavenly Father knows that you need them all. But seek first the kingdom [of God] and his righteousness, and all these things will be given you besides" (Matthew 6:31-33). The world would have us first seek our material goals — financial success, social recognition, power positions, professional prestige — and then offer any residual time to God. God tells us, however, that those priorities are reversed. When we set our first priority to live the will of God, not only will we be happy but also sufficient material gifts will be ours. For those of us who receive abundant material gifts, there is the unique opportunity to share abundantly with the less fortunate.

"Blessed are the merciful, for they will be shown mercy" (Matthew 5:7). Our Lord said when he told us how to pray, "Forgive us our debts, as we forgive our debtors" (Matthew 6:12). If we wish to be forgiven, we must forgive. Our Lord has promised that we will know happiness in forgiving others, and conversely, failing

to forgive others brings unhappiness. How simple it would seem to forgive; we have only our pride and self-centeredness to lose. When we forgive others, we share directly in the life of the Spirit.

"Blessed are the clean of heart, for they will see God" (Matthew 5:8). Our Lord said, "Amen, I say to you, unless you turn and become like children, you will not enter the kingdom of heaven" (Matthew 18:3). In other words, unless we accept and trust God without question, as a child accepts and trusts parental authority, we shall not see God.

"Blessed are the peacemakers, for they will be called children of God" (Matthew 5:9). Those who work for peace will receive peace, for we become what we think. Those who live peace at the very core of their existence will be prophets of peace to the world.

"Blessed are they who are persecuted for the sake of righteousness, for theirs is the kingdom of heaven" (Matthew 5:10). Often, we are afraid to state in public our religious feelings and faith values because we fear people making fun of us. Many of us may even be seriously harassed or physically threatened. Remember that our Lord said, "But whoever denies me before others, I will deny before my heavenly Father" (Matthew 10:33). Public acknowledgment of our Lord is much more difficult for some of us, depending on circumstances. However, the degree of difficulty will have much to do with how we prioritize the spiritual and material aspects of our lives.

Why Have Faith?

What is faith? Some think faith is belief in something that may happen. ("I have faith that I will make a fortune in business.") Others have faith in their own ability to rise above the crowd. Neither is faith. Both are expressions of egotism, a supreme confidence in one's own ability. We see the powerful influence of egotism in the proliferation of books, articles, and seminars on self-esteem. While the formulas for self-confidence may offer some advantage toward material success, they are easily directed away from the joy of spiritual growth.

The type of faith addressed here is not concerned with one's ability but is related to God. Faith is the acceptance of God's truth without scientific proof. Note that I say *scientific proof,* for there is considerably more proof of God than of most things we accept.

Why do we trust or believe anyone? They are a recognized authority. They are known to follow through on promises or responsibilities. They demonstrate a special ability or skill. We trust such as these on the basis of past performance, believing they will speak the truth and produce satisfactory results. For example, we put our lives on the line whenever we board an airplane because we have faith and trust in the pilot, the airplane manufacturer, and airline mechanics.

Then why not have faith in God? Did God not produce many miracles that have never been equaled? Jesus was the prophesier of more than one thousand recorded events that came to pass. Would we not have faith in any human being who could produce such results? Since no other human has ever adequately foretold the future, certainly this ability must be of God.

But all of these proofs, even in the days of Jesus when they could be witnessed firsthand, are not enough. Faith denies proof; human reasoning is not the primary factor. No matter how wise, learned, or educated we become, we cannot reason our way to God. If we could, a privileged few would earn their way to heaven by intellectual pursuits while enjoying an elitist relationship with God. The rest of us would be lost.

The "proof of God" for those of us who are Thomases comes as we witness the gifts of inner joy, deep peace, and fulfillment that can originate from nowhere else but Pure Goodness. It is a basic truth of life that the result of knowing and living the will of God as revealed in Scripture brings happiness and contentment unequaled by any other act.

It would seem, therefore, that the question "Why have faith?" makes more sense if it is revised to "Why not have faith?" If faith offers greater peace and the hope of an eternal reward, why not pursue faith with vigor, persistence, and without reservation?

Unfortunately, many of us don't realize that the happiness of faith is better than any other type of belief. Often, it takes us a lifetime to come to this conclusion. For many of us, this realization dawns when we get in touch with our own mortality. For a few, the gift of faith comes early in life, and they are blessed. For most of us, however, it comes after some experience of life and the disenchantment of the material struggle. Then, when the noise of the world is turned down, the quiet voice of the

Spirit within can finally be heard. In any event, we must practice faith as though we had it; in God's time it will be ours.

Pleasure and Joy

E veryone wants to be happy, but few know the experience. We don't know the difference between pleasure and joy. Joy gives happiness because it comes from within, is of God, and lasts as long as we meet our intrinsic needs. Joy is not controlled by anything outside of ourselves but by belief in the Word of the Lord — which is unchanging. Joy is ours as we attempt to follow our Creator's plan for us. It brings inner peace and comes with a divine assurance that no one can take it from us. Joy does not make us jaded. Each level of joy is sufficient, requiring no higher level of intensity. Greater measures of joy bring an exhilaration unequaled by any pleasure. Joy leaves no regrets, side effects, depression, or longing. Our Lord said, "I have told you this so that my joy might be in you" (John 15:11).

On the other hand, pleasure is from without and depends on someone or something external to ourselves. Pleasure is fleeting. Because of the nature of things on which pleasure depends, a rush of pleasure is always followed by disappointment and depression. Pleasure is a seeking of various stimuli, each requiring a higher level of intensity to avoid being jaded.

Pleasure is built on self-seeking efforts while joy is built on self-sacrifice. Pleasure requires constant exhilaration; joy is satisfied with quiet fullness. The priority list for obtaining joy is always the same: love God, love others, love yourself.

The Ultimate Choice

W e each determine our own emotional universe. We have within ourselves the potential for perpetual sunlight and constant joy regardless of our life circumstances. It's a matter of choice. Those who freely posit their personality in accordance with nature and direct their life toward God know the depths of lasting joy.

Unfortunately, many of us choose to look outward for this, to external events that will provide a temporary high. Since no one can control external events, these people are destined to be disappointed. A glut of entertainment becomes boring; a passionate romance loses its thrill. The pleasure does not endure.

What endures is joy, the joy that is ours when our intrinsic needs are met. The frustrations and complexities of life no longer control our moods. We level out as we travel the peaks and valleys of daily living. Our moods become balanced on the constancy of joy. We choose to align our priorities with our natural goodness — and we come to know life more abundantly, as promised by Jesus. (See John 10:10.)

Chapter II

Intrinsic Need 2: To Live a Meaningful Life

Pursuing Life's Purpose

Jesus' thoughts were directed toward his life plan: fulfilling the prophecies of the Scriptures and completing the mission set by his Father. For us to be happy, we must be as conscientious about meeting our own need to fulfill a worthy life plan. Our Creator has a master plan for all creation. Every plant, star, animal, human being, and galaxy is part of a natural order.

It would be inconsistent with the order of nature to think that humans are not in harmony with our Creator's plan. Yet we are all unique; we each have our special gifts, our own levels of awareness, and our own place in creation. Spending time on things inconsistent with our purpose will leave us feeling empty.

All of us have a life purpose, a reason for living, a purpose that gives direction to our goals and our life's mission. These goals are not destinations in and of themselves; they're milestones along the journey. When our goals are not consistent with our purpose, we fail to know a sense of fulfillment. When a self-serving goal of fame or fortune is pursued, we remain unsettled and disillusioned; we lack inner peace. Many propose that goals should be revised along the way to prevent actually reaching them, thus generating a constant challenge. But this practice is self-limiting, similar to that experienced by pleasure seekers who need each experience to increase in intensity to prevent jading and disillusionment. Unfortunately, many of us won't realize this until we're faced with despair and emptiness. How tragic. Meeting goals that are not consistent with our life's purpose results in frustration and loss of precious time.

The ultimate purpose of life is to glorify God. This purpose may be accomplished in many ways: through our loving, being loved, and serving others. By attempting to fulfill our intrinsic needs, we glorify God because we fulfill our Creator-designed purpose. The specifics of how we fulfill our intrinsic needs are not crucial. In fact, if we find ourselves lavished with fame and fortune as a by-product, fine; we have the challenging privilege of serving others in truly unique ways.

Since we're only as successful as we think we are, however, our plan of action must be of our own choosing, not imposed on us by others. Human beings have a basic need for freedom; free will is at the core of our humanness. If our free will is restricted, we cannot fulfill our life's purpose. As we move through life, we exercise our free will to determine our goals and how we will meet them. We also have the very life of God within to inform our choices: grace.

As We Think, We Are

As we gain life experiences and come into contact with others, we begin to realize that most people simply put up with life and take the path of least resistance. We also notice that most people are not really happy. Paychecks, weekends, vacations, and countless other dimensions of life serve as escapes from a deep and painful emptiness. Most of us spend the greater part of our lives resigned to accepting whatever comes our way and reacting with complaints about how everything is someone else's fault.

Generally, we notice what's wrong with people, society, situations, ourselves. Read the newspapers and magazines and listen to the nightly news. What interests people? misery and other people's problems. What are our usual responses? "Well, I'm not alone. Other people have problems too" or "I really don't know how lucky I am." The conclusion one tends to draw is "I'm not in control of my life. Other people and circumstances determine everything about my life." We take what comes into our lives and either complain or resignedly accept by pulling away like a kicked puppy.

Why are we like this? We are a negative-thinking people. We're a suffering, complaining, unhappy people because of the way we think. We bring discontent on ourselves — not intentionally, of course. But the way we think influences all of life. If we think we're under the control of another person, group, set of circumstances — we are. If we think today will be a drag, unpleasant, unproductive — it will. If we think we'll fail a test of our intellectual, physical, or emotional attributes — we will. The sum of our lives is the sum of the choices we make by the way we think. Science has long determined that we direct our own destinies — and Scripture reinforces this. Our Lord said what you sow, you shall reap. (See Galatians 6:7.) In other words, if you think negatively, negative things will happen.

Can we change? Let's be honest. Most of us are unhappy a good deal of the time, yet all of us would put happiness at the top of our wish list. Realizing that we're the way we think, the obvious questions are "Can we change what we think? Do we have the power and means to change our thinking so we will expect good things to happen to us? Is this realistic? Can the weakest of us — those of us with little initiative or will power, those of us who are marginally coping with life's problems and have no reserve strength left — have any hope whatsoever for happiness?" Maybe the overachievers can make major lifestyle changes, but for most of us, just getting through the day exhausts our energy. In fact, reading this book may be a major effort for some of us.

Can we change? The answer is a resounding yes. Not only can we change our thinking, but we're commanded to do so by Jesus. His message is one of repentance, of turning away from sinful ways and turning toward God. Changing our ways necessitates changing our thinking.

Because God has commanded us to change, it is possible. The strength and the way are within reach of each of us. It is not a new and revolutionary scientific-psychological breakthrough, no secret and long-hidden meditation, no brain trick involving illusions. The way is revealed in Scripture and the strength is offered to us by our Lord. Much of it has been preached to us for generations.

Despite its availability over the years, however, the way is difficult for those of little faith; it's hard to trust. Too, it has been obscured by the thousands of viewpoints of ministers and preachers who have a lot of space and time to fill with words. Its simplicity often gets covered with religious verbiage.

What is it? *Think like Jesus and you will be like Jesus.* The strength to do this is available to all by connecting with our Lord. Our conscious acts of love will put our subconscious in touch with the Spirit, and the power of the Spirit will enable us to change our way of thinking.

Think Like Jesus?

D oes this seem like an unrealistic goal? In the absolute sense, it is. But only a small percentage of Jesus' happiness is needed to improve our present lot significantly. It's a goal to work toward, each step improving our lives. After all, we can only measure happiness in a relative sense. We're happy when we think we're happy, and we think we're happy when we feel better about ourselves than we did yesterday. If we can think even a little like Jesus, we realize significant spiritual growth and improved perspectives on life.

How did Jesus think? Jesus thought with love. Jesus frequently reminds us that we have the power to change the way we think. "The kingdom of God is among you" (Luke 17:21). Within us lies the power of self-healing, happiness, and peace of mind. We tap it by starting to think like our Lord, by loving others, by loving ourselves.

Self-love

L ove was Jesus' principal credo. The Scriptures teach that we cannot love our neighbor until we love ourselves; obviously, self-love must come first. This is where we start to fulfill our own needs. We can't change the world, but we can change our own lives, beginning with our inner world. To love ourselves genuinely is not a self-serving attitude but something we must accomplish before we're able to love God and others.

Positive Thinking

J esus is the definition of positive thinking. His teachings of love can only be followed by a positive attitude, since repentance and faith can only grow in a positive mind and heart. Jesus' life, death, and resurrection is our promise of redemption, of an eternity of peace. He left us his peace and the Holy Spirit to comfort us, to bring us that peace here and now. Our Creator fashioned in each of us a conscience to help us discern options and choices. And to top it all off, God favored us with unconditional love as a foundation for our faith and a free will to exercise in the acceptance of that love.

Practically speaking, what does positive thinking mean? It means that in our perception of reality, we try to see good in every situation. If the good isn't immediately evident, we trust it to be made manifest in the future. For example, after an accident and the initial grief that follows, we can always find the positive aspects. This doesn't mean that we callously laugh in the face of misfortune; rather, we steadily concentrate on the positive. A positive attitude does not look for problems but searches for opportunity.

Interdependence and Positive Thinking

J esus was not dependent on others. He relied on himself, his Father, and the generous goodness of others. He also welcomed those who needed to rely on his healing strength. This is interdependence. Dependent persons allow people and circumstances to provide them happiness, to give them direction. They follow in blind obedience and are at the mercy of others. Many of us have been taught since childhood to depend on others for our well-being; consequently, when problems beset us, we complain that others have let us down.

Until we eliminate dependence and embrace healthy interdependence, we will never assume responsibility for our own lives and make those changes required for the fulfilling life God intends for us. Jesus thought positively and took responsibility for his life; he never complained about others making his life difficult. In fact, Scripture would lead us to assume that he never complained. He made himself available to others while accepting the goodness of others — all the while believing in the unconditional love of his Father to provide life's basic needs. That's faithful positive thinking.

Beyond Average

M any of us are perfectly willing to be satisfied with "average." In our childhood, decisions were made for us by our parents. As we grew away from their protection and guidance and had to begin making some of our own decisions, we became fearful; we didn't know how to trust our own thinking. When we were forced into a decision, we likely conformed to popular notions and simple solutions. If the quality of our lives is the sum total of our choices or decisions, and all the decisions are average and determined by popular notions, what are we? who are we? With time, we discard any chance we might have to invest our talents and our "talents." (See the Parable of Talents, Matthew 25:14-30.)

Jesus always used his gifts to the maximum. He never conformed to convention. We might say, "Well, that was easy for him; he was God." Yes, but he was also fully human and, as such, subject to the same anxieties we are. He knew the sting of rejection and ridicule. He drew on his human strength to transcend the pain, to stretch himself beyond the average response. He embraced the reality of the moment and consciously chose his Father.

The Reality of the Moment

N o two people have the same awareness. Your awareness includes your background, life experiences, values, beliefs, desires, and assumptions. Reality is the total level of your present awareness. In other words, reality is relative and "in the eye of the beholder." It is much the same as truth, since reality is essentially the truth of the matter. All human truth is ever-changing and subject to individual perceptions. God's truth, on the other hand, is absolute and never-changing.

We can only be at peace with ourselves if we accept and respect our own reality and the reality of others. Most emotional problems are caused by resisting our own or someone else's reality. Jesus accepted the reality of the moment. He accepted that which he could not (would not) immediately change but was patient until circumstances changed. When he first taught at the synagogue (Luke 2:41-52) and his parents found him, he accepted the reality of the moment and put himself under their direction. As the often-quoted prayer goes: "God, grant me the serenity to accept the things I cannot change, the courage to change the things I can, and the wisdom to know the difference."

Accepting another's right to his or her sense of reality eliminates judgmental thinking. If we accept the fact that another perceives his or her reality in accordance with his or her awareness, we'll have no basis for harsh judgments. Jesus clearly instructs us not to judge others.

Those of us who cannot accept the reality of the moment will suffer in proportion to our degree of resistance. Accepting the reality of the moment was basic to Saint Paul. He wrote, "In every circumstance and in all things I have learned the secret of being well fed and of going hungry, of living in abundance and of being in need" (Philippians 4:12). We must allow ourselves and others the freedom of their personal reality based on their awareness. We must not judge others by our set of values, nor can we judge ourselves as being good or bad, right or wrong. We can only do the best we can with what we have to work with. Jesus teaches this. The outcome of our decisions and actions is not the measuring rod; only our intention and efforts are of merit.

Think Love

S aint Paul wrote, "So faith, hope, love remain, these three; but the greatest of these is love" (1 Corinthians 13:13). Perhaps even more to the point is John's straightforward insistence: "God is love" (1 John 4:16). Scripture teaches that love is everything: "But [if I] do not have love, I am nothing" (1 Corinthians 13:2). So think in loving ways, do acts of charity, practice goodness. As you consciously think love, you will subconsciously accept and reflect Jesus' unconditional love for others and for yourself.

Unconditional love, however, requires self-knowledge and self-understanding. How we view ourselves, our self-image, has everything to do with how we think — and remember, "As we think, we are." Our happiness, success, and failure are preconditioned by our self-image. If the mental picture we have of ourself is that of an unsuccessful person, we will think in ways that ensure failure. Not consciously, of course, but we act out the portrait of our self-image. If we had an unhappy, loveless childhood, our self-image might be that of a person unworthy of love; throughout life we might be unable to love others because we cannot love ourself. Our self-image pictures a person who is unlovable and, therefore, unable to give love.

One way to think of self-image is as a script for a part we play on life's stage. If the script doesn't get changed, we must continually act the part out. The script is in the form of mental pictures we have of ourselves, formed by life experiences and personal reality awareness. If our self-image pictures an unhappy person, we're guaranteed unhappiness. Outside conscious acts — material possessions, associates, toys, games, parties, food, drink — may give momentary pleasure in our pursuit of happiness. Many of us spend the majority of our lives seeking these perceived pleasures. None, however, will produce even a small percentage of the happiness derived from a positive self-image.

The psychology of self-image is not a new concept; it has long been documented and accepted by the medical profession. Controversial discussion centers around methods by which we *change* self-image. Although many books and articles have been written on a variety of methods, Jesus remains the primary teacher and model of a positive self-image.

Reconstructing Our Self-image

Jesus' message to the world was to repent: turn from sin and turn to God. Since our self-image largely determines how we think and what we do, repenting requires a self-image revision. Our three basic needs that must be fulfilled in order to ensure happiness also require self-image revision. To accept God's unconditional love, we must see ourselves as lovable and loved.

To picture ourselves as capable of completing our life plan, we must see ourselves as capable of wise and responsible choices. Even to meet body-care needs, we must view our body as worthy of that special care.

Jesus teaches, "You shall love your neighbor as yourself" (Matthew 22:39). To love ourselves requires a good self-image. Knowing that we are created in God's image is to acknowledge our own goodness and immense intrinsic worth. For many of us, achieving a sense of self-worth is going to mean effort and change.

Making the Change

As we get closer to God by fulfilling our intrinsic needs, we are able to accept more of God's love — which in turn allows us to better love ourselves. This is basic in revising our self-image. Positive thinking is a result of a positive self-image and ensures the optimum use of our God-given gifts. We can will ourselves to think positively, but without a positive self-image, we won't convince ourselves for very long. There are key directives for effecting a change in our self-image.

Celebrate individuality. Measuring ourselves against others is not only an injustice and limitation to our own goodness, but also it develops a falsehood. When we take our cues of identity and value from another, we deny the authentic goodness of our own personhood. We are all gifted in different measures, designed to think and act in ways reflective of who we are at our core. To think and act in other ways is to impose on ourselves a heavy burden: the forming of a person we were not fashioned to become.

Accept imperfections. To live a mistake-free existence is to exclude our humanness. Our mistakes are our direct path toward growth; they are our tools for building tomorrow's success.

When we were babies learning how to walk, we fell. This was not considered failure, however. With each tumble, we developed better motor skills, a greater sense of balance, and greater courage.

There is no shame in making mistakes — unless we fail to learn from them or fail to persist in our goals. Time after time Jesus taught persistence, wearing away obstacles by unwavering determination. He totally accepted the imperfections of the world around him.

Maintain balance. Building and strengthening our self-image is crucial to fulfilling our life purpose. Keep in mind, however, that our energies cannot be focused exclusively in pursuit of this end. We have other needs that cannot be overshadowed. We put peace of mind and soul at risk in emphasizing an improved self-image while neglecting our other needs. Our needs must all be met in harmony with one another.

Be realistic. To change and maintain a healthy self-image, we must be realistic. We have to know our limitations — limitations that even the most powerful and successful must acknowledge. Life's experiences will indicate to us our physical and mental breaking points, points at which the pressure causes us to think irrationally and respond negatively.

Don't heap abuse on yourself for these limitations; be realistic. Self-criticism serves no useful purpose. In fact, self-attacks only increase limitations by generating negative thinking. Punishing one's self for mistakes or limitations tears down self-image.

Establish goals. To give our lives purpose, we must set goals — realistic goals. For most of us, this means short-term goals. We need to focus our activity on some goal we feel will give us a sense of accomplishment. Without careful planning of these goals and careful reflection on their being reached, there is no means to measure our progress. A sense of movement to complete our mission in life is essential to meeting Intrinsic Need 2.

Foster friendships. "No man is an island" declares a well-known adage. None of us exists in a vacuum independent from all those around us. Our lives revolve around our relationships with other people: interdependence. Intrinsic Need 1 requires us to express our love to others. Love in this sense is brotherly love, caring about the quality of life of our brothers and sisters. This need for friendship is essential to each of us with varying intensity.

We're back to self-love; we can't form friendships unless we first like ourselves. Friendship is no more than a form of brotherly love. These friendships involve genuine concern for others as compared to using acquaintances to further self-interests.

The quickest way to develop friends is by getting interested in other people rather than trying to get them interested in you. Nothing wins friends so much as an unselfish concern for others' needs. The ability to form long-lasting friendships has much to do with the quality of our self-image. If you don't like yourself, chances are others won't like you either.

Develop positive attitudes. There has been much said and written about the advantages of having a positive attitude and the power of positive thinking. A large number of articles and books has been written and seminars have been held on this technique of self-improvement. The potential lies within each of us if only we activate its mechanism. How to be happy and how to feel good about yourself are the results of this attitude. Health, by whatever biochemical transformation, improves when the mind has a positive attitude — a kind of self-fulfilling prophecy in which we think ourselves healthy.

We're all familiar with stories of terminally ill people who make miraculous recoveries that can't be explained by the medical world. What is this undefined power that the mind has over our success in health, wealth, and happiness? It's the simple application of a positive mental attitude.

To be complete and permanent, however, positive thinking must be empowered by the Spirit. Although some can cause a positive motion by a temporary act of will, a complete positive outlook can only come through faith in the work of God. By its nature, the condition of the Spirit is totally positive, which is the essence of hope.

And what is a positive attitude other than the hope that all things will get better?

"The lamp of the body is the eye. If your eye is sound, your whole body will be filled with light" (Matthew 6:22). In other words, what you see is what you are. If you see health and happiness and you have faith, the Spirit will empower you to move in that direction. If you have a negative attitude and see only failure and bad things, those things will come to pass. A positive attitude must stem from a good self-image. One cannot will good things for any length of time without genuinely liking oneself.

For this reason, our level of success cannot exceed the level of our self-image. And since self-image equals self-love, we must believe we are lovable.

Obviously, a good self-image and a positive attitude are not the first steps to happiness. Rather, meeting Intrinsic Need 1 (love) by accepting God's love results in a good self-image and a positive attitude that shape our thinking for happiness. In meeting Intrinsic Need 1, we are better equipped to meet Intrinsic Need 2: fulfilling life's purpose.

Accept God's love. We can will our minds to think positively about ourselves, but we must really believe it. That belief comes through acceptance of God's love. Knowing that we are not perfect yet are loved unconditionally allows us to trust in God's generous care. We will always doubt to some degree. But in God we can trust; we must trust. God's love for us has been made manifest in the life of Jesus, God's beloved Son.

Spirit in a Material World

When we were young, most of us were obsessed with the materialism of the world. We were handed materialistic values from our parents and watched others exert their efforts toward acquiring things and displaying their successes in our competitive world.

Youth is a period of concentrating on the things that personify our personalities: electronic appliances, high-performance automobiles, elegant homes, novelty toys, tailored clothing. Conversations center on elite vacation resorts, good real-estate buys, profitable investments. For most of us, the first half of life revolves around how many of the world's treasures we can obtain.

Then comes midlife. For most of us, midlife is the time we start to realize that life does end at some point; we're not immortal. This realization is probably the most traumatic of our lives. To finally accept that death will occur to us in the not-too-distant future is a jolting experience. Our thinking is forced into realigning our goals and values. What's important in life gets a new name; materialism transforms to spiritualism. We come to understand that we're more than a job, a house, a bank account. The proximity of death is the catalyst that changes our life's values.

Once the end is in sight, materialism no longer covers up our real needs. After all, what could be our motive for wanting things that have an eternal value of zero? We learn this lesson by pursuing the treasures of the world, by making materialism our god. While there is goodness in the basic comforts of the world — health-care, shelter, rest, adequate diet — commercialism has ballooned our perceived needs out of proportion. When the stark realization of death appears, most of us finally realize that this world's treasures eventually rust or pass on to others. It is here that Intrinsic Need 2 kicks in with a profound invitation: do something worthwhile for humankind. People realize that attempting to meet their needs in the material world leaves them with only fleeting or no emotional satisfaction; their basic intrinsic needs are not material based.

Materialism is also perceived by some as an answer to deep-rooted fears: loneliness, not having a meaningful place in society, aging, death. While materialism is by far humankind's most popular need satisfier, the fact remains that it is a poor second to the real satisfier: the Holy Spirit.

So What Is Spiritual?

We can't discern it directly with our senses, but most of us have our answer. Certainly, it is mysterious; it's an energy. This energy in relationship with God is called the Holy Spirit.

We know that the Spirit of our Lord is essential to our salvation. As Jesus said, "No one can enter the kingdom of God without being born of water and Spirit" (John 3:5). We can further describe the Holy Spirit characteristically: "The fruit of the Spirit is love, joy, peace, patience, kindness, generosity, faithfulness, gentleness, self-control" (Galatians 5:22-23).

Webster's Dictionary has many definitions of spirit. The root word means "to breathe," and its first definition is "animating or vital principle held to give life to physical organisms." Another definition is "a supernatural being or essence."

Scripture, however, describes Spirit as "God within us." Spirituality is often affiliated with the constant conflict between the flesh and the Spirit (the essence or Word of God). For our purposes, this meaning of *Spirit* — the essence of God — is the one we use throughout this book.

Make Room for the Spirit

Upon his departure from the world, Jesus left us the comfort of his Holy Spirit. The Spirit is available to guide and protect us, to be our solace in loneliness, our joy in goodness, and our means to inner peace.

How do we communicate and leave ourselves open to the Spirit's guidance? We begin by embracing silence. We turn off the noisy distractions of our competitive and anxiety-laden world and enter into the silence to listen, meditate, and pray. Any communication requires listening as well as talking. If we don't listen to the voice within us, we can't communicate. Quiet time apart from the thundering din of the world is critical to our happiness. To prepare for the experience of quiet, our ego must be suppressed.

The ego is a control maniac; it craves control. On the other hand, acceptance of the Spirit plunges the ego into silence, stripping it of all control. The ego's obsession with materialism is the enemy of the Spirit. Materialism sufficient to meet our basic creature needs is good. Beyond that, however, obsession with materialism masks the first two human intrinsic needs and prevents their fulfillment.

Silencing Through Meditation

A way to embrace silence and connect with God is through withdrawal from the world to focus on one's being. Meditation is a means toward this end. The purpose of spiritual meditation is to communicate with the Spirit. It quiets the ego to receive inner messages from the subconscious mind that stimulates a bonding with the Spirit. Meditation nourishes inner peace by enjoyment of the moment without worry of guilt from the past or fear of the future. Most importantly, meditation removes the restrictions of our minds to the higher levels of awareness of the Spirit and the Spirit's ability to empower us to meet our intrinsic needs.

A question remains, however: how does an average person, beset by the demands of life and endowed with various mixtures of awareness and ingrained habits, get sufficiently motivated to pursue quiet, to cultivate an awareness of the Spirit, to reform old comfortable habits into new untested ones? How does one begin?

First, quiet and meditation must become part of your daily schedule. Relax. Even if only in your mind, leave behind the worldly concerns that press in on you from all sides. Refresh yourself. Prepare a part of yourself to receive an inner joy that glorifies God.

A simple technique for achieving this quiet involves the selection of a word or short phrase, preferably from Scripture ("God is love" or "Jesus"). Sit in a comfortable position where you won't be disturbed. Close your eyes, relax your muscles, and breathe naturally. As you exhale, picture the word or phrase. Make no effort to think. Extinguish thoughts that enter the mind by focusing on the word or phrase.

Continue this process for approximately five to ten minutes. Initially, don't be concerned about the depth or length of your meditation. Practice will enrich this habit. With time, you will relax; a peacefulness will settle in along with the ability to discard some of the negative thinking that has been a millstone around your neck. After meditating, when the mind is quiet, pray; communicate with the Lord. There are countless ways to pray. Other than a few guidelines mentioned in Scripture, your form of prayer is whatever works best for you.

The Mind and Faith

Although the experience of meditation calls for a quieting of the mind, the mind does not play a significant role in deepening our spirituality through faith. Prayer and meditation provide means for reaching deeper levels of faith. We prepare ourselves, body and mind, by training, discipline, and perseverance — and our spirituality takes shape.

One theory on the beginnings of spirituality has to do with human evolution. About ten thousand years before Christ, humans started to reason and make decisions. They needed an inner voice to guide their reasons and decisions. The inner voices were thought to be divine commands, and thus the beginnings of religion took root. Early Scripture characters fell into this category and were thought to be divinely directed.

Another theory regarding spirituality has it that spirituality is a neurochemical process that explains the spiritual experiences of consciousness. The effect of deep prayer, meditation, and exercise on certain brain chemicals results in a type of religious or emotional ecstasy.

A third theory endorses the theological premise that the brain cannot grasp the immensity of the cosmos, that there is no physiological reason for the need for human spirituality.

We do know that a part of the mind is associated with a part of the brain that contains a belief system not logically explained, that is more experienced than expressed. While the left hemisphere of the brain is associated with logic, analysis, and verbal description, spirituality is centered in the right hemisphere and cannot be easily described. Right-hemisphere thought transcends our consciousness to reach a spiritual space.

How much of this process can be explained in physiological or biological terms by future researchers is, frankly, not of much concern. Whether our spiritual activity takes place within our mind or is a voice from elsewhere makes little difference. We are concerned with happiness. The advance in scientific knowledge concerning the mind will never eliminate the very real experience of faith. For if we could scientifically prove God's existence, there would be no purpose for free will, and the glorification of our Creator would be robotic and meaningless.

Don't wait for — or even desire — scientific proof or miracles. Rather, deepen your faith by prayer and meditation, acts of goodness and love, and care of your body. Happiness awaits you. The spiritual joy you'll discover is sufficient personal proof of God's love.

The Mind, Faith – and Tragedy

Let us return to the question of misfortune and tragedy. What is the answer to the unfairness in life? Why do the immoral prosper and the moral suffer? Why does a self-centered person enjoy good health while a loving, self-giving person lives a life of chronic illness? Why do some people seem always happy and full of life and others withdrawn and despondent?

The exercise of our mind and our faith does not allow us to sit passively back and be satisfied with half-baked answers to these questions. Yet the concept is basic: that one person is happy and another is not has to do with fulfilling our Creator-designed needs. That one person is successful and another is not, by material measurements, has much to do with the way we think, as described in the section "As We Think, We Are" in this chapter.

Our conscious and subconscious have the power to

improve our lives far beyond what we may dream. Toward this end, the mind joins faith in forming our future. Through the Son, our Creator promised that our prayers will be answered in faith. We've already established that our thinking can operate as a self-fulfilling prophecy, that whatever we believe we are, we will become. In the same way, the answer to prayer results when our subconscious mind responds to the thought or picture of our conscious mind. The subconscious mind is scripturally defined as that which is in our heart. Periods of quiet meditation open the space for faithful prayer — prayer that defines and determines the fulfillment of our heart's desires.

The Subconscious Mind

Scripture implies that the subconscious mind operates on our system of beliefs. Jesus said, "Have faith in God. Amen, I say to you, whoever says to this mountain, 'Be lifted up and thrown into the sea,' and does not doubt in his heart but believes that what he says will happen, it shall be done for him" (Mark 11:22-24). The functions of the conscious and the subconscious mind are two different processes. The conscious functions as the waking mind; the subconscious functions in the relaxed or sleeping mind.

Many definitions and schools of thought are involved with the mind and its functions. Since there is no scientific definition available, opinions abound. For our purposes, definitions are based on scriptural interpretation.

The theory professed in this book is that the mind is similar to a program for a computer, which is the brain. The mind has two basic sections, one for each hemisphere of the brain. The conscious mind is the section of the program primarily taking place in the left hemisphere of the brain. It is concerned with logic, language, and so on. The section of the program that concerns the right hemisphere, or creative functions, is the subconscious part of the program. That which is scripturally referred to as the "heart's desire" comes from the subconscious section of the program. Communication with our God through prayer is effected by the subconscious.

These two sections of the program are further connected by a feedback loop that allows the subconscious program to change according to the nature of the program (thoughts) in the conscious program. To empower our subconscious to desire God's will, we must consciously think and follow God's teachings; we must consciously choose periods of quiet and meditation. After all, the program that controls our brain was fashioned by our Creator to give our lives order. This program is essentially the same for all humans and explains why we have the same basic needs which, when fulfilled, result in genuine and lasting happiness.

Unfortunately, confusion over how to fulfill these needs and how to exercise our free will makes happiness more desired than acquired. It is the inner world of the mind that empowers us to change our circumstances. Most people, however, try to alter the conditions of their lives by manipulation, trying to change outer circumstances. In reality, outer circumstances are merely the effect of an inner cause.

To change your outer life, the cause must first be changed — that is, your thinking and mental imagery must change. For example, if you're lonely, eliminate the cause of loneliness in your mind rather than attempting to get close to everyone you meet. Think of yourself as a lovable person, see yourself as God sees you: precious. Think of yourself as valuable, which you are. Follow some daily routines such as spiritual meditation and prayer. Become peaceful. Practice acts of goodness to accept God's love; you will, in turn, reflect this love to others. Once the cause of loneliness, the inner you, is changed, your subconscious and conscious mind will cause your outer life to change.

The conscious mind controlled by your free will is essentially the captain of your heart (the subconscious mind). When the conscious repeatedly tells you that you can't do something, the subconscious picks up on this and feeds it back twenty-four hours a day at an intensity proportional to the alertness of the conscious. This process ensures that you won't be able to do the thing you said you couldn't do.

An example of this subconscious operation might be waking early for some special event. Prior to sleep, the conscious mind is told repeatedly that you can't oversleep or you'll miss the meeting. The subconscious mind picks up the commands from mind control and feeds them back all night: "Don't oversleep or you'll be late." Consequently, you get little or no sleep as you wake every hour to look at the clock. The cause is your inner self — your mind's thoughts — and the effect is a change in your outer circumstances, namely, no sleep.

The subconscious is the center of your emotions and is the creative part of the mind. If you think in terms of failure and shortcomings, failure and shortcomings eventually rule your life. If you think in loving ways, your mind will work in ways that direct your efforts and talents in a positive direction. The conscious mind is rational and handles all the decision-making programs; the subconscious mind is irrational and makes no decisions. It is directed by the conscious mind and works behind the scenes without effort; it simply carries out the instructions of the conscious mind. The subconscious has no value system and accepts equally that which is positive or negative. It accepts without judgment whatever your conscious believes.

In addition, your subconscious is programmed to carry out certain body functions — breathing, circulation, digestion — without any conscious effort on your part. However, the thoughts of the conscious can modify the subconscious program for body functions to a degree proportional to an individual's ability to control his or her mind within designed limits.

A common example of the irrational design of the subconscious is demonstrated by the ability of a hypnotist to make a suggestion and have the subject perform any number of completely irrational acts. The subject's subconscious receives the commands from the hypnotist in the same way it would from the conscious; the subject acts to carry out the commands regardless of how irrational they may be.

The conscious mind has its input through the senses and learns by experience, observation, and education. Its most important function is reasoning. On the other hand, the subconscious mind does not have direct input through the senses and is not able to reason. It is the location of emotion and memory. Its special abilities are demonstrated when the conscious mind is relaxed during meditation, prayer, or sleep. During this time, communication with the Spirit within is done via the subconscious mind. It is for this reason that meditation and prayer are essential; distractions being processed by the conscious mind are stopped by meditation and prayer. Channels for spiritual communication are opened.

The idea is to affect the conscious mind by acts of meditation, prayer, goodness, and love directed toward fulfilling our intrinsic needs. Our subconscious mind will then function to move us in the direction of our "heart's desire": happiness.

Chapter III

Intrinsic Need 3: To Care for the Body

Health and Mind

When your body is uncomfortable or in pain, it's difficult to be happy. And since happiness is the focus of this book, the condition of the body is of major importance. Because happiness is basically spiritual with a thin coating of materialism and creature comforts, one can be partially happy, spiritually happy, while the body is uncomfortable or feeling bad. For all but a few of the saintliest individuals, however, a body condition that is not distracting us from meeting our spiritual needs is mandatory.

Consequently, safeguarding our health is a high priority to enhance need fulfillment, and toward that end, the relationship that the mind has with the body plays a significant role. Medical practitioners admit that present scientific remedies are helpful in only about a third of the patients they treat. The other two thirds have a mind/body relationship, or they improve on their own. Many medical articles indicate there is a mind/body relationship that affects anxiety attacks, migraine headaches, asthma, phobias, high blood pressure, various body pains, ulcers, and hypertension.

Unfortunately, mind/body relationships are scientifically unknown in most situations, yet there is a high probability that the relationship is responsible for many medically unexplained cures. Scripture and present-day reports abound with such accounts. Faith-healing demonstrations fill our television channels and newspaper headlines. How much of this is showmanship is unknown, but there is mind/body relationship on display wherever we choose to look. Most of us know ordinary people who have been cured of an illness without a medical explanation.

There is no question that the mind plays a part in the wellness of the body. To what degree? under what circumstances? These are the questions.

The Temple of the Spirit

God is immanent. "Do you not know that you are the temple of God, and that the Spirit of God dwells in you? If anyone destroys God's temple, God will destroy that person; for the temple of God, which you are, is holy" (1 Corinthians 3:16-17). God has admonished us to take care of this temple.

What's more, we know that body care is an intrinsic need for happiness. Medical and psychological research have amply demonstrated that a proper diet and adequate exercise are crucial to our overall well-being. Anyone involved in an exercise program knows its positive effects. On the other side of the coin, anything under our control that adversely affects the health of the body offends the goodness of God, not to mention the offense to those who love us.

Anything unhealthy to the body reduces the expectation of happiness. Media information on unhealthy habits (smoking, drugs, overeating, undereating, overexercising, underexercising) barrages us. Our faith, scientific research, our culture, and our common sense tell us that body care is essential to happiness.

Taking Care of the Temple

I t is well understood that the wholeness of the person is contingent upon the bonding of the mind and body. Although the body is under the control of the mind, it maintains a feeling of well-being when properly cared for. The mind is then free from the distractions of pain and suffering. Simple programs designed for the care and maintenance of our bodies are well publicized and accessible to most of us. Although the body was designed to operate over an extremely wide range of environmental conditions, uses, and fuels, there are, however, optimum conditions that maximize its performance and service to life.

The Need for Balance

A s you proceed through the following sections, keep in mind the principle of balance. Everything in moderation is a basic principle of the universe. The components of the universe need to have equal and opposing forces to maintain its state of equilibrium. Likewise, we need a balance in all things to be in harmony with the natural laws of our Creator. We have been fashioned to require a certain amount of exercise, a certain amount and type of food, the right amount and quality of sleep, the proper amount of mental exercise and relaxation, sufficient spiritual fulfillment, adequate love, and enough meaning and purpose in our lives.

These are basic needs that the dignity of our human condition requires. When we don't meet these basic needs, when we neglect some needs or are extreme in others, we get out of balance and lose a sense of well-being.

Our bodies have a feedback system that tells us when we're in balance. A feeling of well-being, physically and emotionally, is normally the best indicator. When we feel good and like ourselves, we're usually meeting our intrinsic needs.

Sufficient Exercise

It has long been known that exercise promotes a feeling of well-being and requires both physical and mental conditioning. In the not-too-distant past, a strong physical condition was more important than mental prowess. We lived a rugged physical life in keeping with nature's selection of letting the strong live and the weak perish. Then came the industrial revolution, and machines virtually eliminated humankind's need for physical strength.

More recently, the technological revolution has almost eliminated physical fitness as a job requirement. For many of us, the body's chief task is to carry around and support the brain. This technological revolution has also freed humans to enjoy an unprecedented amount of leisure time. With this available time we can devote our creative energies to improving the quality of life. Health now becomes an important aspect. That, coupled with recent medical research, has made exercise trendy. Two thirds of the young and over fifty percent of the total population of the United States work out in one way or another. Some research even suggests that our lives can be extended by a few years; other research concludes that aerobic exercise strengthens the heart and circulatory system.

Regular exercise of the proper intensity and duration also develops collateral vessels that can reduce the damage caused by heart attack; it may even prevent an attack. Other studies show the reduction of high blood pressure through regular exercise. A correlation between exercise and an increase in the amount of protective HDL (high-density lipoprotein) has also been validated by research. This is explained in greater detail later in this chapter.

Exercise should be an important part of weight control and stress reduction as well. With regard to weight control, exercise increases the metabolism which in turn burns calories long after the period of exercise ceases. For marathon and long-distance runners, it's almost impossible to eat enough to gain weight. The calories burned in carrying one's body weight a certain distance in a certain length of time are just part of the total increase in calories burned in a regular program of exercise.

It is widely accepted that stress is a risk factor of heart attack. Exercise has demonstrated the ability to relieve pent-up stress. Many of us know that feeling of well-being and relaxation that follows sufficient exercise.

The positive benefits of exercise are substantial. What are the negative characteristics? The possibility of injury is probably the most serious drawback. However, this possibility is greatly reduced provided we follow an exercise program designed by a knowledgeable authority. Jumping into an exercise program without medical approval and without experienced guidance is not wise and can result in injury. Many of us know of someone who "overdid it" and caused herself or himself physical damage. Fortunately, the gurus of exercise insist on limited exercise — the result of injuries caused by overemphasizing exercise some years ago. Other drawbacks of exercise include time and inconvenience.

There are a number of well-researched and time-honored exercise plans that provide sufficient detail for most persons. After fifteen years on an exercise program, I know and enjoy a feeling of vibrant bodily well-being. I've heard this same thing from countless other exercise devotees.

Prior to this period of dedicated exercise, from age twenty to forty, mine was a sedentary life, devoid of exercise. During those years, I had a much lower energy level and rarely had a feeling of physical well-being. Although the exact amounts and benefits of exercise are controversial, there is little question that some exercise is imperative for our sense of well-being.

Sensible Exercise

R ecent medical research confirms, to no one's surprise, that excessive exercise increases the risk of injury. For most of us, "a training effect" (the point at which a maximum amount of oxygen is carried to all parts of the body) can be achieved in less than forty-five minutes of aerobic activity three or four times a week. For some, a twenty-minute period is sufficient. Above that level, additional exercise doesn't provide equivalent benefits; for some, it can cause injury. Government studies on large groups of runners indicate that a significant number have quit or reduced their running due to injuries; similar results are evidenced in other high-impact aerobic exercises. Any orthopedic specialist can tell you of the increase in tendinitis, ligament sprains, stress fractures, bone spurs, shin splints, pulled muscles, and other injuries caused by excessive exercise. My own experience with overexercising bears this out.

About fifteen years ago I was impressed with articles on aerobic exercise. Lured by the professed health benefits, particularly regarding heart disease, I began a jogging program. I had long been a Type A workaholic, and it was well publicized that Type A personalities were at higher risk for heart attacks. Since I hadn't had any significant exercise since my early twenties, some twenty years earlier, I started a program.

My initial jogging was a city block at a time. Over the first year, my distance and speed increased. With time, my motives for jogging shifted from physical benefits to the simple fact that jogging made me feel good. It was an outlet for stress, and I felt more relaxed than I had in years.

When a few of my friends became interested in jogging, we started to run together on a daily basis. As ego would have it, our jogging soon became competitive; we found ourselves running longer and pushing for speed, all in the interest of training for the Boston marathon — or so we convinced ourselves. After a year of this rigor, some of us were running seventy miles a week: about ten seven-minute miles each weekday and twenty miles on weekends. We were spurred on by articles in magazines and books testifying to the fact that anyone who could run a three-hour marathon was immune to heart attacks. At that time, very little medical research on the negative side of exercise was shared with the public.

Similar to a dope addict, the jogging addict requires a daily fix of a quick five or ten miles or else the body rebels; the jogger is riddled with excess energy. Everything in the body cries for an exercise fix. For me, the end was inevitable. After years of living for running — even to the point of my business deteriorating due to lack of productive time on the job — nature pulled the plug. The heels of my feet became so painful I could hardly run. Yet every fiber in my body egged me on — and I continued to run. Eventually, my heel became painful to the point of limiting ordinary walking.

The orthopedic surgeon took x-rays and found large bone spurs. No problem to the surgeon. They could be sawed off, and after six months in casts, I would again walk without pain. But would spurs develop when I began running again? The surgeon couldn't say.

Just prior to this time, I had injured my back by trying to handle a barbell heavier than I could realistically manage. Running only aggravated my back problem, a pain that limited my sitting, tennis playing, golfing, weightlifting, and so on. I decided against the surgery on the theory that the spine is more important than the foot.

The moral of this story? Anything done to excess — including exercise — eventually results in problems.

Getting Started

I f you're over forty, overweight, smoke, have a family history of heart disease, or have high cholesterol or high blood pressure, you should have a complete physical with a stress test. To start retraining your body, select an exercise program that is slow and easy. This caution is crucial and cannot be overstressed. Your body may not have seen exercise for more years than you care to think about. Any quick starts could have bad consequences. Set your goal for the level that provides maximum oxygen distribution without overstressing your musculoskeletal system.

The amount of effort and time needed to reach this point will depend on your physical conditioning or lack of it. The approximate heart rate for you is 220 minus your age. For instance, if you are forty years old, the maximum heart rate for you is 180. Never exceed this rate during exercise.

Next, multiply your maximum rate by both sixty and seventy-five percent; the range between sixty and seventy-five percent is where you should get your heart rate during exercise. Check your pulse during and after exercise and adjust the exercise level to keep it in your range. Select an exercise that allows you to increase your heart rate to your range without risk of injury.

The American Heart Association publishes a chart

that graphically displays the desired range of your heart rate. The goal is to adjust your energy intensity to get your pulse within the target zone by way of an exercise that is least likely to cause injuries. The simplest way to check your heart rate is on the coronary artery alongside your Adam's apple. Count pulses for ten seconds and multiply by six. No matter what exercise you select, remember to start slowly and increase in stages, each stage lasting long enough to ensure training or conditioning of the body at that level. This should be the basis of any good program recommended by a recognized medical authority on exercise.

Obviously, if the exercise is enjoyable and convenient, it will be easier to make it a habit. You may be better off avoiding high-impact exercises such as running, aerobic dancing, or jumping rope. Brisk walking is a more sensible choice, provided you can reach your desired heart rate. Swimming is also a good choice for a low-impact, high-intensity exercise.

For those who insist on high-impact exercise, proper conditioning and shoes are essential. There are many complete exercise programs available that provide all the details you need. Also, there is an increasing number of medical facilities that publish exercise programs or have their own fitness centers.

In any event, the exercise must become a habit performed at least three times a week to obtain lasting cardiovascular fitness.

Very recent studies by researchers at the Stanford University School of Medicine indicate that there isn't sufficient evidence to determine whether an exercise stress test can reduce the heart attack rate for patients planning to begin a program of fitness such as running or jogging. Your best way to reduce any exercise risk after you have your physician's go-ahead is not to exceed your maximum heart rate, start at low levels of intensity until your body becomes conditioned, and avoid high-impact exercise as much as possible.

A Proper Diet

A well-balanced diet, low in fat, sugar, and salt, is important to a fit body. Many extreme methods abound; appealing plans of weight loss and control proliferate. There exist all kinds of opportunities to be thrown out of balance in this area. The potential side effects of some of these unique weight-loss and weight-control plans are simply not worth the risk. Professionally researched and proven diets, such as those published by the American Heart Association, are usually sufficient for both a well-balanced diet and weight control. Those with special problems are advised to consult a competent health professional before taking on one of the newly touted methods of weight control.

Stress

M uch scientific evidence indicates that the stress of today's lifestyles exacts a considerable toll on our emotional and physical health. *Webster's Dictionary* defines stress as "a physical, chemical, or emotional factor that causes bodily or mental tension and may be a factor in disease causation."

Worries and anxieties are intensified by tension that blocks meditation, relaxation, positive thinking, loving thoughts, and happiness. Severe stress will prevent our movement in the positive direction of well-being.

Consequently, stress is to be minimized. Avoid situations that you know cause you stress; emphasize daily meditation and prayer. In many cases, this also reduces body pain. Meditation, positive thinking, and prayer reduce and eliminate pain if it is mind/body related. Of course, pain that has an obvious direct physical cause — toothaches, severe burns, abrasions — should be attended to by a medical professional; make this a standard routine whenever there is doubt regarding pain.

In fact, when you become ill, physically or emotionally, or when you're considering a diet, experiencing stress, or decide to quit smoking, a licensed medical professional should be your first stop. Where the professional cannot help, your mind can. How the mind/body relationship works is unknown; whether faith healing is miraculous or not is uncertain in many cases. But the connection between mind and body is a fact. There is no question that physical and emotional illness can be cured without scientific medical explanation. Since the power of faith is unlimited by our restricted scientific boundaries, we must believe that our own personhood is still being formed in the pain at hand.

A Healthy Heart

C ardiovascular disease is the leading cause of death. This disease involves the clogging of the arteries of the heart and other vital organs. Because of the overwhelming numbers of Americans who suffer cardiovascular diseases, federal and private medical research has intensified in recent years. The development of coronary-care units, the heart-lung pump, heart-rhythm drugs, electronic heart pacemakers, and improved medical procedures have meant life for many. Mortality from heart attack has been significantly reduced, but a preventive measure is obviously a better answer.

Research during the sixties discovered the three major risk factors of coronary heart disease: cigarette smoking, high blood pressure, and elevated levels of blood cholesterol. When these characteristics are present, a person has ten times a greater risk of having heart disease. As a result of the widespread dissemination of this information, a large segment of the public has developed a healthy lifestyle; deaths associated with cardiovascular diseases have significantly decreased in recent decades. This disease, however, is still our number one killer. What can we do for ourselves now?

Blood pressure: Blood pressure can be controlled by maintaining body weight, reducing sodium intake, and taking medication if necessary. Check with your doctor, have your blood pressure checked on a regular basis, and follow the advice of professionals. They know what you need to do today to ensure your health for tomorrow.

Cigarettes: Smoking can be stopped by an act of will. Tobacco use fell thirty percent, and over forty million Americans stopped smoking between 1963 and 1977.

A wide variety of reliable programs is available to help you stop smoking. Basically, however, you must want to quit — and the basic motivation to break this offensive habit is found in love. In accepting God's love and loving ourselves, we take the best care of God's temple. We know smoking desecrates and destroys this temple. By sacrificing a sometimes pleasurable, more often unpleasant habit, we claim good health for ourselves.

These risk factors, of course, are statistical; we're all familiar with exceptions. There are those who have ignored or have been ignorant of the risks involved in smoking and have lived in apparent good health to a ripe old age. There is no guarantee that changing one's lifestyle in accordance with the current health statistics will prevent an early disability or death. But the odds are more in your favor!

Cholesterol: The control of cholesterol is a more difficult preventive measure to effect because it requires a basic change in our lifelong eating habits. Since eating is a universal pleasure, we are obviously reluctant to consider changes that seem unappetizing. The basic problem lies in the fact that the majority of us are accustomed to eating foods that have a forty- to fifty-percent fat content. This type of eating, however, is nothing more than a habit formed over the years. In reality, the body has no need for high levels of fat.

Total cholesterol can be broken down into a number of fractions: low-density lipoprotein cholesterol (LDL), very-low-density lipoprotein cholesterol (VLDL), and high-density lipoprotein cholesterol (HDL). LDL is generally thought to be the cause of deposits in the arteries leading to coronary heart disease. VLDL is referred to as the "bad cholesterol." The "good cholesterol," HDL, operates to pull cholesterol away from the linings of the arteries.

The higher the HDL, therefore, the greater is the protection against heart disease. While data can be presented to show the risk of heart disease as being related to cholesterol levels, we each have to make our own decisions.

In 1987 the federal government and many health organizations issued the latest guidelines for physicians and the public. They all agreed that serum cholesterol levels should not exceed 200 mg/dl for anyone — a substantial reduction from previous standards.

According to authorities, diet is the first means of reducing cholesterol. For those not responding to diet modification, drugs may be necessary. Cholesterol reduction to under 200 mg/dl is no longer controversial. It is now in the same category as smoking and seat belts. It's simply the right thing to do. Medical research also suggests a second guideline regarding the ratio of total cholesterol divided by HDL cholesterol, which should be less than 4.5.

There are many books available about cholesterol control that discuss balanced diets and provide tasty recipes and calorie counters for those interested.

Weight: We live in a society that is weight conscious. Many of us are aware of the extent to which our weight dramatically affects our ability to function in ways our Creator intended. Overweight and underweight people generally have low self-images due to lack of self-love; they are not motivated to care for their bodies. To be happy, we must love ourselves — which means fulfilling our intrinsic need of love. As we work at fulfilling our intrinsic needs, body care takes on a whole new perspective. It is not an end in itself but part of a process of glorifying God.

Fortunately, a bonus to cholesterol control is weight reduction. Since fats contain more calories than equivalent amounts of complex carbohydrates, weight can be reduced without hunger pangs. Unfortunately for the already thin, an increased food intake is necessary if body weight is to be maintained.

As always, consult a physician before launching into serious weight-control programs. Rates of weight gain and loss must be carefully monitored for a weight program to be effective and healthy.

You Can Change

D eciding to reduce health risks is an intelligent and spiritual choice. There are no guarantees, of course. The current evidence regarding healthy habits may be developed further in the future; research is ongoing. Certain measures may not work for you, but the efforts are worth the possible benefits. With the facts we do know, it is illogical and irresponsible to disregard opportunities which result in the good of your overall well-being.

Use the power of your mind to change your habits. Rather than thinking of going on a diet, for example, think of a permanent change in your eating habits. After all, what you eat is an acquired habit. You were not born with a preference for bacon and eggs; this is a developed habit. If you were born in England, your preference could just as well have been steak and kidney pie. Think about retraining your taste buds to enjoy low-fat foods. Once you get used to foods low in fat, salt, and sugar, you'll develop new habits and enjoy your meals more knowing they're as wholesome as they are delicious.

This same retraining of the mind holds true for smoking. Think about the smoke-free environment you'll enjoy. Your clothes, hair, furniture, and draperies will not be coated with the stale odor of cigarette smoke. Your tastebuds return, and eating becomes a time of discovery. You save money; you save the environment; you safeguard your health.

Medical research has revealed countless abuses that humankind can launch against itself. Jesus taught us to repent of these "sins" against the body, the temple of the Spirit. Use your love of self, others, and God to gain respect for your body. Tap into the power of your mind and exercise positive thinking. Respect your intrinsic need for body care.

Chapter IV

Practicing Happiness

A Daily Schedule

T o move in the direction of happiness, a regular daily schedule is crucial. This involves redirecting our lifestyle in ways that generate new habits. Only when we change our conditioned reflexes and ingrained habits, however, will we adopt a different lifestyle. For example, many diets do not produce satisfactory results because individuals fail to take this approach. They fail to form new habits, which means the diet must be forced by will. Since it requires a special effort and is not an automatic response, the diet soon falls by the wayside. Generally, we all take the most comfortable direction; we're creatures of our habits.

But we know we can change. Our Creator sent his only begotten Son into this world to deliver the message of repentance: "If you do not repent, you will all perish as they did!" (Luke 13:3). Jesus challenges us to turn away from sin and toward God. Obviously, this would have been a pointless message if we were incapable of changing our thinking and replacing old habits. We're fashioned with the ability to revise our lifestyles. This is demonstrated countless times in Scripture and by the lives of saints and martyrs. There are billions of people who have changed in the name of Christianity. Change is not only possible, but God passionately longs for it. God desires our happiness.

Making a significant alteration in lifestyle, however, is a massive undertaking, too large for most of us to accomplish quickly. Large undertakings seem too formidable at first glance. The challenge must be broken down into more realistic goals. It's like climbing a mountain; the mountain shrinks to a series of small easily attainable goals if it's taken one step at a time. Likewise, the following goals will become manageable when they're taken individually and performed every day — every day. This will not be easy. The ever-present invitation from commercialism and materialism rings in our ears. We become easily absorbed in building our future by upgrading our properties, exercising our influence, or just surviving. Eventually, there is no time for spiritual meditation or deep personal growth. Meeting our intrinsic needs gets lost in the mayhem.

Then, when we're faced with our own mortality, our frantic preoccupation with the things of this world comes to an end. There are no distractions. The things we've spent a lifetime collecting are gone, and we stand naked before the Lord. How have we glorified God in our life choices?

Goals for Daily Happiness

The basic guidelines for change are revealed in Scripture: a healthy self-image, responsibility, positive thinking, kindness. Since these scriptural truths are God-inspired, they are accepted in faith as truth. Later writers, expounding on similar topics from a secular base, have come up with other methods of life improvement. Permanent change, however, cannot be made without the strength of the Holy Spirit. The premise of this book is inspired by this ancient and life-giving wisdom.

The following rules are essential to the happiness plan. If these become ingrained daily habits, a new life of happiness is yours. If not, your efforts will be in vain; you'll gradually fall behind the walls of your previous confinement.

1. Spend at least fifteen minutes in prayer and spiritual meditation.
2. Do a good deed or perform a special service for someone else.
3. Live each day as though it were your last.
4. Upgrade your self-image; you're a precious child of God.
5. Will positive thinking.
6. Do your job to the best of your ability.
7. Set aside time to relax.
8. Spend at least thirty minutes on body care.
9. Set and fulfill daily goals.
10. Do something fun; we never outgrow our need to play.

These are the major ingredients in effecting life-style changes, changes that generate happiness in proportion to effort. You may develop your own special techniques, but here are practical suggestions for getting started.

1. Prayer and spiritual meditation: Prayer and meditation are perhaps the best methods for turning our attention to God. For our purposes, prayer is a form of conversation with God that may be uttered aloud or in silence, in a group or in solitude.

Spiritual meditation is a deep form of prayer by which we remove ourselves from all distractions to communicate with the Spirit through our subconscious mind. To do this, intense concentration is required along with a relaxation of the body and an emptying of the mind. Properly done, spiritual meditation can bring a tremendous sense of well-being and peace — the joy of being closer to the Lord.

When we reach a point of high stress and feel the panic of anxieties or worries, release is necessary to relieve the tension. For those who practice the techniques found in other sections of this book, meditation is one of the best ways to accomplish this. Meditation is the cornerstone of happiness and peace. It's vital to getting in contact with the Spirit within, the source of all inner joy.

2. Good deeds: Jesus lived a life of service; he set the example for us. Service to others can be developed in several ways, one of which is simply to make a goal of doing at least one good deed every day. This deed must be for the good of another and performed with no reward or payback in mind. Practicing this form of life becomes increasingly easier and soon turns into joy — effortless joy. Good deeds flourish into virtues, virtues spawn holiness, and we open up to accept the unconditional love of God.

3. Live each day: The Scriptures teach us to live each day as though it were our last; we never know when it will be. To live a self-centered, self-serving life with plans to repent at the last moment is the height of folly.

This kind of existence only ensures a life of sadness and suffering, loneliness and ultimate despair. So live each day fulfilling your intrinsic needs; live a life of happiness with joyous anticipation of being with our Lord.

4. Self-image: Take every opportunity to upgrade your belief in yourself. When occasions arise that erode your self-image — someone says something uncomplimentary about you or you fail at some task — give careful and objective thought to the situation before you turn on yourself.

We are created in God's image. God doesn't care about our limitations and failures. God desires only our best and most loving efforts. If our thoughts and actions are with the Spirit, we know our intrinsic worth. The judgments of others do not speak to us of our worth. If our worth were, indeed, contingent on the perspective of others, we would forever be miserable creatures. Our worth would fluctuate from one contact to the next. To have authentic meaning, self-image must be rooted in the truth of intrinsic worth. My self-worth must come from within myself, as I understand myself and know myself as a child of God, living the Word of God as I understand it.

5. Positive thinking: Positive thinking turns every problem into an opportunity. It allows us to see that some eventual good is part of every circumstance — *every* circumstance. We each have a reality based on our individual awareness; we can embrace a positive position independent of another's reality. Negative thinking provides no benefits, does absolutely nothing constructive, and moves us in a direction away from happiness.

6. *Do your job:* Work is part of the human experience. Jesus was a common carpenter. Likewise, the apostles had their livelihoods in addition to their teaching. Work is basic to the Christian life; few of us can pass the day in idleness and live the Christian life. Earning our keep is necessary for a good self-image; providing for ourselves and our families is fashioned in the human mind and is an important part of Intrinsic Need 2. The nature of the work itself is not the issue; rather the work must produce an awareness that our basic intrinsic need is being fulfilled.

7. *Relaxation:* Our bodies and minds require periods of rest and relaxation. For this, our Lord said we should take one day in seven. Some of us require more time, some less. Clinical research shows the adverse effects of too little rest. Obviously, we can't be happy when we're in a state of mental or physical exhaustion. By the same token, too much sleep does not leave us at our best. Necessary body care must be undertaken to establish a balance. Set aside extra time each day to refresh yourself; do something restful. Take a walk, read a book, indulge in a nap, meditate. Do whatever works for you.

8. *Body care:* Three areas are of prime concern: exercise, diet, and rest. We've already addressed the details of these concerns. It's difficult to be happy when the

body and mind are not at peace. A tranquil mind and an uncomplaining body are essential to a state of spiritual meditation and meeting Intrinsic Needs 1 and 2. There are those who can transcend physical limitations by a highly trained and saintly mind. Most of us, however, are not capable of such transcendence; we have to rely on more routine means of taking care of ourselves. All humans, from the most talented to the least gifted, have the same intrinsic needs; it's only the quantity of these needs that differs.

9. Goals: Throughout this book, we've emphasized the necessity and techniques for goal-setting. Living by objectives is a practical method for most of us to progress in a desired direction. Our major objectives in life often get lost in day-to-day "fire drills." Small goals performed daily toward our major objectives allows us to take control of our lives rather than just reacting to the circumstances of the moment.

10. Fun: Most of us make life so much more unpleasant than it needs to be. Why be so serious? Our Lord said that we will not enter heaven unless we are like little children. Playfulness describes the nature of children. The need for fun is part of the human makeup; we don't outgrow it. It makes us feel good, and often it is an unreserved expression of love. Fun should be positive, other directed, and never to the disadvantage of others. It need not call for any major financial outlay. In fact, the simpler, the better. Having fun meeting our intrinsic needs is another method of realizing the happiness we desire — and are entitled to.

Keep Score

The table below will help you monitor your daily goals. Some type of habit-forming method is necessary to make your thinking automatic.

Daily Happiness Goals   **Week Starting** _____

Goal	Minutes, Yes or No						
	M	Tu	W	Th	F	Sa	Su
1. Prayer and meditation	10	15	10	5	10	5	10
2. Good deeds							
3. Live each day							
4. Self-image							
5. Positive thinking							
6. Job							
7. Relaxation							
8. Body care							
9. Goals							
10. Fun							

The above displays a partly completed chart. As happiness habits become ingrained, your chart will become more positive. As joy becomes more a part of your life, the goals will become habits — good habits. The chart will no longer be necessary.

A Monthly Checkup

T o reduce backsliding, it's important to monitor your progress. Any time is fine as long as it allows for adequate reflection and becomes a part of the routine. When starting the plan, a daily review is useful. Once progress is made, a weekly review will suffice. Gradually, you'll need only a monthly review.

In this review, ask yourself, "Am I happier than I was before I started this routine?" If so, then you're probably moving in the right direction. Then, assess your rate of progress. Is it up to your expectations? If not, review your goals and list your daily, weekly, monthly, yearly, and life goals. Your daily goals should include the ten goals for daily happiness. Review all checkmarks to see if you've developed a daily habit that easily becomes weekly and monthly. If so, review some of the preceding comments regarding each goal. Gain a better understanding of and appreciation for the goal. Prepare a monthly chart similar to the daily chart. This will help you determine where you need greater discipline. Open yourself to the strength of the Spirit to help you make progress.

The most reliable means for measuring your happiness is you. If you think you're happier than before you began reading this book and living its directives, then you know success. You're moving in the right direction. The rest is up to you. The taste of happiness will increase your appetite for more. God's love is like that; there is never a saturation point. We're left with a desire for more — always.

Chapter V

Support and Inspiration

Treasures of Lasting Value

As a lasting treasure, I offer you some final thoughts. Success of the happiness plan is rooted in these basics.

Everyone wants to be happy. We may each take separate routes, but we pursue the same end: happiness. Humankind's basic nature is to pursue happiness. No matter the goals to which one aspires — power, wealth, sex, fame, goodness, honesty, righteousness, love — happiness and joy are our ultimate desires.

Happiness is not a state of being; it's a condition of becoming. It's relative. We're either happier or sadder than we were five minutes ago, yesterday, or some years past. What's more, happiness has different levels of satisfaction for different people. Many of us are satisfied with some feeling of happiness during a small part of our waking time. Others seek happiness to the point of obsession.

Does wealth produce the happiness that modern commercialism would have us believe? Many of us spend our lives pursuing it only to find that the object of our pursuit evades us. Yes, wealth can be obtained, but if at the price of happiness, it's worthless.

Wealth is not synonymous with happiness. If wealth is our god, we will reap the consequences of serving an idol that ensures a life of sadness. History gives us many examples of the wealthy and their lives of suffering.

Fame, honor, and glory fit into the same category.

Like wealth, they bring momentary pleasure and then fade or cause an ever-increasing drive for more.

None of these pleasures are bad in themselves except when we seek to make them an end in themselves. "Seek first the kingdom [of God] and his righteousness, and all these things will be given you besides," said our Lord (Matthew 6:33). Ironically, by seeking wealth, fame, and glory as their own ends, we pay the price of sadness; by seeking first the kingdom of God, we discover joy and happiness — perhaps with sufficient or abundant wealth added to it. This is not to say that we shouldn't use our God-given talents for the best return; rather, the wealth is to be used for the glory of God.

Peaks and Valleys

Peaks and valleys are normal conditions of life. Emotionl and spiritual ups and down are experienced by all of us regardless of economic, social, or spiritual status. If we find ourselves in a valley, it doesn't mean we're being punished. A valley is an opportunity for us to practice our faith. For through adversity we sharpen our perseverance skills — skills essential in the crises of life.

We must, however, be in touch with the strength of that inner resolve that will carry us through troubled waters. When we find ourselves in an emotional valley (which is determined by a temporary lack of inner joy), remember a few key components. No matter how mechanical it may seem, perform one or more acts of goodness each day and seek no favors in return. Also, get away by yourself — if only for ten minutes — to pray and meditate. This refuels your inner determination to be happy by seeking help from the Creator of love. Joy is the exhilaration of love, and as we are able to accept more love from God, we're able to give more to others.

The Role of Rest

It is essential to keep the intention of the commandment regarding rest: "On six days work may be done, but the seventh day shall be sacred to you as the sabbath of complete rest to the LORD" (Exodus 35:2). In God's divine plan, we were formed with a need to rest from our worries and troubles, to refresh our spirits by silence, prayer, and meditation. This period of rest and meditation is necessary for our proper functioning. This commandment is not to be taken literally, however, for the following reasons.

First, the Holy Spirit in the Book of Acts moved the day of worship and rest from the seventh day to the first day of the week. Second, God's day is not to be confused with our human-designed day of twenty-four hours. Third, there are those who must work on the sabbath: medical personnel and law enforcement officers, for example. Finally, if we follow this commandment to the letter rather than the Spirit of the law, it could cause more stress than it would relieve. Jesus clarified the purpose of the commandment when he said, "The sabbath was made for man, not man for the sabbath" (Mark 2:27).

All of us have our stress limits which, when exceeded, result in anxieties, a lack of harmony, and an unspiritual perspective. This can cause problems with our family, social life, and working habits. High-stress levels put a damper on our ability to love, and consequently, happiness is blocked. The need for rest, prayer, and meditation varies in quantity and quality from person to person; we must know our needs and set our own requirements. One seventh of a week is only a guideline dependent on individual needs and circumstances.

When we're tense and unable to achieve a degree of inner peace, when a smile doesn't come easily, rest is probably needed. If we don't get the rest we require, tension escalates until our stress limit (defined as the point at which we can no longer experience joy) is reached. When we exceed our limit, we lose control and our judgment becomes irrational. The stress accelerates further until some event results in relief or disaster. Unfortunately, this event is usually a bitter argument, an unpleasant confrontation, or something equally serious. Others become victims when we release our stress in inappropriate ways.

When we're not happy or at peace, we're not meeting our intrinsic needs. Reviewing the daily happiness schedule in the previous chapter will help. For many, meditation is one of the most effective stress relievers. If you're too tense to meditate, use your fists against a pillow or punching bag. (Using our fists in times of high stress seems to be a primal urge.) Such temporary stress relief is possible as long as the target is inanimate.

Another good stress reliever is exercise.

The Role of Acceptance

For most of us, life means some amount of dissatisfaction or suffering. This is a basic reality of life. Most of us spend a great deal of energy complaining about the weather, our jobs, our bosses, our golf games, our children, our spouses, and on and on. Most of us resist these daily unpleasantries, expecting that life should be easy. So much energy is wasted in this resistance.

Whereas, if we accept the reality that life is not perfect, that we're not perfect, that others aren't perfect, suffering and discontent no longer seem important or worth complaining about. We face life with the understanding that things simply are not neat, tidy, and forever comfortable.

Jesus taught acceptance. He taught that acceptance of pain, suffering, and disappointment is a way to endure and transcend the situation. For eventual good, Saint Paul was content in all situations: prison cells, the frustration of waiting, the hardships of journeys, and celebrations with friends.

Life is an endless series of choices. We have the option to face our problems with the positive viewpoint of acceptance or the negative viewpoint of resistance. Many decisions involve suffering as well as pleasure.

Obedience to God's word is the technique we use to make these decisions. When difficult choices must be made, God's law is the only constant justification for our repeated positive acceptance of suffering. When we truly accept God's love, we find joy.

Therefore, be content in suffering for a better good; not only will you do something of value, but you will also strengthen your will for even greater challenges.

When life is viewed with a negative attitude, we see only problems, no opportunities. Naturally, this puts us in a defensive stance; we want to avoid or escape unpleasantries. But this viewpoint leaves little opportunity for mental or spiritual growth; it forms a defensive posture of self-containment. The positive viewpoint of seeing life as a series of opportunities, however, is outgoing, open, and loving. It is concerned with the possibilities of faith, wholeness, and joy.

Responsibility

Too many of us suffer from a character disorder or a neurosis resulting from too much or too little responsibility. Those with character disorders assume that their problems are everybody else's responsibility; those with neuroses assume that everything is their responsibility, that when a problem arises, it's their fault.

When problems are viewed as opportunities, however, fault is no longer an issue. The healthy Christian takes responsibility for choices in the immediate moment, knowing that a positive influence is adequate in any situation. For most of us, the difficulty we have in accepting appropriate responsibility lies in the desire to avoid any discomfort or anguish we perceive associated with that responsibility.

Caution, however. Do not let self-blame be your motivation to take healthy responsibility. In early childhood we begin to emphasize certain personality traits. There are many theories about why we do this. Was our environment a loving home or was it laden with tension? Who were our heroes? What values were we given to model? What were the genetic influences? These factors impact our decisions to respond in certain ways — consciously or subconsciously. We responded on extremely limited information and without any significant life experiences for reference. This, combined with whatever environmental circumstance we were in, was the basis for emphasizing a particular trait. As we developed this trait, usually to defend ourselves against some real or imagined problem, it became an automatic response. This style of response formed our perceived self and determined our sense of responsibility.

Since these traits were developed with inadequate input and were probably maintained as a defense mechanism, they're likely unnatural traits based on negative thinking. They're unhealthy. They will not help us determine appropriate responsibilities.

We all have these negative traits. We need to isolate them, remove them from our lives, and replace them with positive habits. While we're in the process of doing this, however, we must keep in mind the background of their formation. We are not to blame ourselves for their existence. If, once they're identified, we allow them to continue, we will then begin to suffer their oppressive influence.

The Beacon of Truth

A nother essential tool for good decision-making is reality. What's real? What's imagined? What's a personal bias? Daily we are bombarded with the glowy commercialism of a biased sense of reality.

Our own sense of reality is being continually revised as the world around us changes and we make attempts to incorporate those changes. Some are not acceptable, some are. Our decisions are largely influenced by our perception of reality. But our reality changes as we pass through the different stages of life. As children, we're dependent on our parents. We're relatively powerless to make changes or see another reality. As adults, we gain a level of power dependent on our circumstances; we can exert a relative amount of influence to change situations to suit our reality at the moment. Those with great wealth and power can influence change in the lives of many; the poor and powerless have little, if any, such influence. To a certain degree, we become powerless and without influence as we enter old age as well. In making choices based upon our perception of reality, God's Truth must become our bedrock.

The Truth of God is absolute; it never changes. We can all take solace in the absolute Truth of all time, all circumstances: the Truth of the Word of God. This Truth always was, always will be; it is the never-changing Truth for all eternity. When the ever-changing truth or reality of the world becomes incompatible with our own sense of truth, a focus on God's Truth ensures the joy and happiness we pursue.

Dependency Isn't Love

D ependence on another is frequently mistaken for love. As designed by our Creator, love must always involve free choice: our free choice to love God and others. Some of us think we love God because we recognize our dependence on God's generous goodness. But true love for God comes from realizing that we were created in God's divine image, an image of pure love. We love God because God loved us first and gave us the ability to love. God loved us enough to sacrifice his only-begotten Son in atonement for our sins.

So if dependency isn't love, what is it? Some of the most common psychiatric disorders involve extreme forms of dependency. People starved for love continually seek relationships to establish their identities. We all have a need for healthy relationships with our spouses, friends, and acquaintances, but when these relationships take the form of dependency, we move into an unhealthy region. Consequently, love must always be given and received freely, without strings or obligations. Love is concern for the growth of another; dependency is self-centered.

The Purpose of Religion

S ome hold the view that religion is a definition of what people think life is all about. Every recorded culture has formed a religion to explain those things that were beyond logic, that were a function of the sophistication of the people and their individual life experiences.

Simply accepting an inherited religion from our parents ensures passive involvement. It may turn into a deeper involvement, but only when we choose the faith of the religion for ourselves. We must exercise our free choice. The need for religion is basic. It helps human beings explain the unexplainable. It is an answer for uncertainty of eternity.

While religion answers some questions, however, that is not the reason one should embrace a religion. Religion serves as a means to glorify God, our Creator. This is how we fulfill our natural purpose in life — not through some human-conceived scheme that supplies answers to unanswerable questions and makes us feel more comfortable about death.

The Good Life

A ccording to one theory, we discover at an early age that our inner feelings are inconsistent with the world. We conclude that society is in some way hostile to us. As a result, we experience hurt and fear. This alienates us from the world; we withdraw and begin to rely on our own resources for life and growth. We reason that through withdrawal we will avoid the pains of being less than totally accepted. Ultimately, this withdrawal and dependence on self move us farther from God and happiness.

But God wants us to have the good life available to everyone. As always, Jesus is our example. Jesus taught us the way of the good life in some of his last statements: "I have told you this so that my joy might be in you and your joy might be complete" (John 15:11). "Peace I leave with you; my peace I give to you. Not as the world gives do I give it to you. Do not let your hearts be troubled or afraid" (John 14:27). Jesus knew inner joy and lived a life characterized by peace.

Jesus' last words were short and triumphant: "It is finished" (John 19:30). He had carried out God's plan and fulfilled his mission. Likewise, God has a plan for all of us; when we make progress on that plan, we know a deep sense of fulfillment that surpasses the comparatively minor feeling of accomplishment we get from life's challenges: our jobs, hobbies, special interests, and so on. These are the ingredients of the good life: joy, peace, and a genuine sense of accomplishment. These gifts are all internally generated according to God's divine creation and, therefore, are available to all. They are the consequences of inner actions, not outer activities. For that reason, they're never realized in the pursuit of external materialistic things. "Things" give fleeting pleasure and then begin either to bore us or demand unreasonable measures of our time and energy. We become captive to the very things from which we solicited pleasure. Human beings were designed to be free, however, not enslaved by things. We should have things, but we must benefit from them rather than allow them to become our masters. This is freedom; this is the good life. We soar in the Spirit, full of inner joy, a deep peace, and a sense of fulfilling God's plan. The commercially advertised materialistic "good life" doesn't even run a close second.

Remaining Free of Fear

There is a school of thought that proclaims there are only two emotions: love and fear. Our need for love is basic; it is Intrinsic Need 1. We don't need love in order to exist, but it is an essential ingredient in living fully with happiness and joy now and hope for eternity. On the other hand, fear is a product of our imagination. We're born with a few instinctive fears such as falling. The rest are instigated by anxiety and poor self-image.

Fear and its companion hate are the flip side of love. Love is a strong attraction and concern; hate is an aversion or rejection. Love is positive; fear is negative. When love is absent, fear creeps in. When love is present, fear finds no room.

Replacing Old Habits

The mind is like a recorder that keeps replaying our old thoughts and habits. Unless we make the effort to change our way of thinking, we become locked into a cycle of repeating ingrained habits. Every new thought is colored with old thinking.

These old thoughts have to be reprogrammed if bad habits are to be replaced with good habits. Positive thinking must replace negative thinking. Our reality must be drawn from the belief that if we perceive a situation from the positive side, we will think positively and will act responsibly and lovingly. This means banning negative attitudes.

A high priority in the cultivation of positive thinking is the exercise of forgiveness. Unforgiveness is negative, produces nothing of value, causes suffering to the person who doesn't forgive (but rarely to the target), and prevents the fulfilling of our need for love. Our Lord taught us to pray, "Forgive us our debts, as we forgive our debtors" (Matthew 6:12).

Aim for Happiness

S et happiness as a goal for yourself. By meeting your three intrinsic needs, happiness will be yours. Only when you live a full life of love, mission fulfillment, and body care will you be truly happy. Without these three ingredients, happiness is not possible. To be loved and to love, to realize that our lives have meaning, and to enjoy the basic pleasures of proper body care: these needs must be met in a balanced way. A sense of worldly achievement will not bring happiness.

Perpetual Motion

The basic law of physics states that nothing will stay in motion without energy to make up for that which is lost. This also applies in the material world. What is given away is lost; additional resources must be added to keep things going.

The physics of love voids this law, however. What we give in love, we receive back in full measure. Love is the perpetual motion of the spiritual world. The initial supply of love given by our Creator lasts forever and grows in proportion to what we give away. For each measure we give, we receive like measure from our Creator, plus an additional amount returned from the recipient of our love. The quicker we give it away unconditionally, the quicker it returns. Why wait. Give love away as fast as you can.

Peace Within

Our inner peace is determined by the way we choose to think. If we have a good self-image and choose to think positively, we will act in ways that reflect goodness. Problems and disappointments do not undermine inner peace unless we react to them defensively. We must view external problems through the eyes of love, for love is our only reality. Out of the essence of love, our Creator has provided the way to our earthly joy and eternal peace. Let us not reject the gift.

Personal
Reflections

OTHER HELPFUL RESOURCES FROM LIGUORI PUBLICATIONS

60 Ways to Let Yourself Grow
by Martha Mary McGaw, C.S.J.

This happy, exciting book can help you make the most of the precious gift of life — every day! Each page presents an idea or suggestion to help the reader open up to life. Each page also includes free space for creating a personal journal. Light and upbeat, yet deeply spiritual and life-affirming. *$2.50*

Scripture-based Solutions to Handling Stress
by Pat King

The author, a mother of ten, writer and speaker, combines scriptural advice, professional research, and her own experience with burnout to create a unique "workbook approach" to handling stress. She helps readers learn how to manage the stress-causing elements in their lives through twelve lessons filled with exercises based on Scripture, prayer, and journaling. *$4.95*

How to Develop a Better Self-image
by Russell M. Abata, C.SS.R., S.T.D.

This beautiful, practical book can lead you to self-discovery — to a greater acceptance of yourself, others, and God. It helps you examine the person your training and feelings want you to be and the person God designed you to become. Through it, you'll come to praise God for one of his finest creations — YOU! *$3.95*

Order from your local bookstore or write to:
Liguori Publications
Box 060, Liguori, MO 63057-9999
For faster service call toll-free 1-800-325-9521, ext. 060.
*(Please add $1.00 for postage and handling
for orders under $5.00; $1.50 for orders over $5.00.)*